The WILLIAM MORGAN AFFAIR

The WILLIAM MORGAN AFFAIR

Masonic Mystery in Upstate New York

ANN WEBSTER BUNCH

Published by The History Press
Charleston, SC
www.historypress.com

First published 2025

Manufactured in the United States

ISBN 9781467155168

Library of Congress Control Number: 2024947390

CONTENTS

INTRODUCTION

This book presents the historical missing person case of William Morgan and explores how the scientific and investigative methods of the day were applied in attempts to resolve it. Morgan's case is placed in its sociopolitical context in order for the reader to understand the public reaction to the bizarre circumstances surrounding his disappearance. This mysterious case comes with eyewitness accounts and purported physical evidence; however, it remains unsolved to this day. Past investigations involved twists and turns, with apparent manipulation of the scientific identification process in 1827 and again in 1881. In 1827, questionable inquest practices resulted in an erroneous positive identification and a subsequent public uproar that spread like wildfire into a national political movement. In 1881, the resurrection of the case helped raise funds for a grandiose cemetery monument dedicated to William Morgan that still stands to this day in the small city of Batavia, New York.

How can the supposed neutral and objective process of science and the analysis of physical evidence result in confounding public and even private reactions? This book explores this question by taking a modern "cold case" investigative approach to available information and evidence related to the Morgan case. In other words, if we knew then what we know now, what would be the results? An empirical and skeptical approach is applied at every step in the process. Empiricism as a philosophical theory proposes that all knowledge originates in experience. Being able to detect something with our own senses allows us to confirm or deny the reports and interpretations of others. We see this as the gold standard for scientists, and recent scholarly work by cognitive scientists such as Itiel Dror shows that even reliance on our senses can be confounded when it comes to decision-making and interpretation based on them. These studies indicate that even scientists who try their best to make objective judgments and decisions are prone to error. For example, one of Dror's studies supplied fingerprint analysts with anonymized sets of fingerprints (which, unbeknownst to the analysts, were actual cases they themselves had analyzed and reported on in the past) and asked the analysts to determine whether these sets represented "matches" (that is, were consistent with one another) or not (no match or inconsistent with one another) or were indeterminate (the analysts were unable to make a decision). Strikingly, four out of five analysts decided differently than they had when they first analyzed the cases.[1]

To counter explicit and tacit biases, a skeptical approach may be applied. Skepticism is an ancient philosophy, like empiricism, that advocates for an attitude of doubt or a disposition to incredulity, either in general or toward a particular object. It proposes that true knowledge or knowledge in a particular area is uncertain. Skeptics recommend the use of suspended judgment, systematic doubt or criticism when one is presented with any information

This book takes the position that a quality investigation relies on direct, empirical, tangible forms of evidence and emphasizes these over hearsay statements and nonphysical and/or indirect forms of evidence. The latter forms are treated with scrutiny and skepticism. We know today that indirect forms of evidence—such as eyewitness accounts—are fraught with problems; for example, the Innocence Project has determined that approximately 70 percent of all wrongful convictions overturned through DNA testing have relied on eyewitness testimony as their main evidence. This book will explore all known leads in the William Morgan case and attempt to contextualize them in order to obtain a better understanding of why citizens in the early half of the nineteenth century—even including a nuclear family member of Morgan's—would be involved with weak and flawed "evidence" of Morgan's supposed death. And why, in the latter half of the century, would the case be brought to the public's attention—ever so briefly—again?

One might view modern forensic science as above reproach, especially if a steady diet of *CSI* and other such television, streaming or published dramas is consumed. Yet today, forensic scientists and investigators realize that they are first and foremost human beings and, like all human beings, have biases in all that they do, some realized and some unconscious. Forensic practitioners today are increasingly taught to take into account their own thoughts and observations in the evidence collection and analysis process. *Human factors* are the conscious and unconscious cognitive biases that all humans have and bring to their daily lives and work. With the help of cognitive scientists such as Dror, forensic specialists have become increasingly aware of these powerful influences and attempt to work consciously to lessen their impact on the analyses they perform and the decisions they make. This book explores the human factors that were undoubtedly working behind the scenes and were influential in the Morgan case.

As members of society, people not only have their own individual cognitive biases but are also influenced constantly by those with whom they live, work and interact. Individual human factors are formed in part by these external group influences. *Groupthink* is a psychological phenomenon that is defined as "the practice of thinking or making decisions as a group in a way that discourages creativity or individual responsibility," according to the American Heritage Dictionary, 5th edition. Sociologists since Émile Durkheim refer to groupthink as a form of collective consciousness. *Conscience collective*, as Durkheim termed it, is the totality of beliefs and sentiments common to the average members of society. Importantly, we will also see that in this case, the power of the printing press was employed to affect these commonly held beliefs and sentiments, with shocking success. Thus, individual biases can become those of the larger group, if the moment is right. And, in circular fashion, these larger-group biases influence individuals' thoughts, opinions and decisions.

Finally, this book seeks resolution, a path forward out of the mists of the nineteenth century. With all its deviations and distractions, will the case of William Morgan ever be solved? Will the (ideally) objective scientific process prevail? Is it a cold case murder—or rather a cold missing persons case of a desperate and troubled man who disappeared, willingly or not, from Upstate New York society? Potential future scientific paths to resolution are described. What better time than the present to topple the (im)pediment of groupthink and confidently rely on clear, unadulterated, valid and reliable scientific evidence to once and for all determine the actual fate of the ever-elusive William Morgan?

Chapter 1

MURDERED OR MISSING?

Never waste the opportunity offered by a good crisis.
—Machiavelli

Anyone passing by the Batavia Cemetery, locally known as Old Cemetery, on Harvester Avenue in the city of Batavia, New York, today will quickly note a thirty-eight-foot-tall monument topped by the figure of a man standing on a pediment overlooking the graves and crypts below with a stance of pride and honor. The granite base that supports this seemingly imposing figure of the past is inscribed on its south side with words that both intrigue and horrify:

> *Sacred to the memory of Wm. Morgan, a native of Virginia, a capt. in the War of 1812, a respectable citizen of Batavia, and a martyr to the freedom of writing, printing and speaking the truth. He was abducted from near this spot in the year 1826 by Freemasons and murdered for revealing the secrets of their order.*

The north, east and west tablets add details to this unsettling inscription. Any curious citizen can get online and follow up on Find a Grave to learn that this Captain William Morgan was born in 1774 and died—as indicated by the inscription—in 1826. His burial is noted to be in this very ground in Batavia Cemetery, with a memorial identification number of 10220283. Thus, both in stone and in our modern-day digital media, an inquisitive

Batavia Cemetery, Harvester Avenue entrance. *Photograph by Steven R. Bunch.*

mind finds seemingly conclusive statements regarding the fate of a man named "Captain" William Morgan.

Yet if one digs below the surface, the clarity fades at once. One will find that there is no body of William Morgan buried in the cemetery grounds, nor is there any actual gravestone of Morgan anywhere in the Old Cemetery. The Find a Grave summary of Morgan's life contradictorily reads:

> *Central figure in the anti-Masonic agitation. His disappearance* and alleged *murder just before publication of his book* Illustrations of Masonry, *an exposé of the secrets of freemasonry, had a profound effect on the politics of the time* [emphasis mine].

Thomas A. Knight, in his 1950 book on this conundrum, refers to the writings on the cemetery monument as "falsehoods graven in stone."[2]

The cloudy memory of William Morgan and his tenuous history with the local Freemasons of the Batavia area is elaborated on in the Holland Land Office Museum, located just a short distance away from his grandiose Old Cemetery statue. The story of the mysterious man's disappearance is detailed there with much less certainty regarding Morgan's fate than the inscriptions on the nineteenth-century cemetery monument.

Farther west, in the hamlet of Appleton, tales of Morgan's ghost live on. A legend from a family-owned winery, Marjim Manor, reveals a haunted history in which a rock from the Niagara River was somehow tied to the drowning and/or disappearance of Morgan. According to the story, Shubal and Sophia Merritt bought the Appleton property from the Holland Land Company in 1834 and built Appleton Hall soon thereafter. Lewis, the son of Shubal and Sophia, created a rock garden, or rockery, there and took that particular rock from its original riverine position and moved it to the winery grounds. This action apparently disturbed Morgan's ghost, who came looking for "his stone" and was sighted near it or the garden on numerous occasions. It is said that Lewis continued to move the stone within the garden, which contributed to the ghost's ongoing distress. Lewis, unfortunately, was shot and killed accidentally by his own father. Thus, the stone was no longer moved around, and visits from Morgan's ghost then ceased. According to a local news story from 2020, however, some of William Morgan's descendants have reported that they feel his presence at the manor. Since ghost hunting is not counted among the numerous scientifically based forensic specialties, this "lead" will be left for others for follow-up.

A cemetery monument, museum displays, even ghost stories reflect the murder or the questionable death of this deceptive personage. So why is the record uncorrected in the twenty-first century, where the all-respected application of investigative science has improved to the point where many methods and instruments are so advanced that they are declared to be the "next generation"? Why, at first glance, does it appear that William

Opposite: South inscription on Morgan Monument base.

Above: Morgan Monument facing south-southwest (*left*) and east (*right*). *Photographs by Steven R. Bunch.*

Morgan was in fact murdered and buried in 1826 near the monument dedicated ceremoniously many years later, in 1882? Why is the uncertainty of his case not clearly reflected in the public record? The answer, in short, as George Orwell stated in 1944, is that "history is written by the winners." A related corollary comes from the Greek philosopher Plato: "Your silence gives consent."

The case of "Captain" William Morgan is an example of a narrative based on hearsay and conjecture taking hold and becoming reified to the exclusion of actual facts and hard evidence, which were ignored or never even sought. The narrative was, for whatever reason, easier to "float," better or more acceptable for someone or some group, more convenient for some and/or more "palatable" to the consumer of the information—that is, the general public. However, the lack of empirical justification for the words

Opposite: Morgan Monument with fresh flowers adorning its base.

Above: Holland Land Office today. *Photographs by Steven R. Bunch.*

that are literally etched in stone and seen online (for the less skeptical and critically oriented, the modern-day equivalent of being "written in stone") begs for evidence, facts and ultimately, if possible, final closure based on these things.

If there is no body located in Old Cemetery in Batavia that belongs to "Captain" William Morgan—and in truth, no remains have ever been found that have been identified as such—the case is technically, from a modern, professional investigative viewpoint, an open missing persons case. Given the time that has passed, we know William Morgan is dead. Yet we know almost nothing about how, when and where his death occurred. Can anything be added today, almost two centuries later, to elucidate our understanding and strengthen the record with facts?

This book will take an in-depth look at the information that is available in the historical record and proceed from there, taking a modern investigative, scientific and fact-based approach to this very cold missing persons case. The cemetery monument references the "truth" that those who erected it desired to express; let us concur that (1) there is a truth that has yet to be determined in this case, and (2) the ideal method of finding the truth involves empirical evidence. We will see that, even with hard evidence, the "truth" can be quite illusory. Layers of interpretation and

Marjim Manor Winery, Appleton, New York. *Photograph by Steven R. Bunch.*

the passage of time obfuscate facts and require skepticism and scrutiny on the part of the investigator. Nonetheless, let us start at the beginning as modern investigators do, gathering facts about the missing person in order to understand the context in which that person disappeared.

A missing persons case typically begins with a report that someone is "missing"—in other words, not where they are supposed to be. When a person is reported missing today, there is not necessarily an immediate reaction by law enforcement and/or investigators. These professionals must first understand specific information about the missing person in order to react appropriately. For example, if the person reported missing is an adult, the response by law enforcement will be measured, considering that the adult may actually *wish* to be "missing" and likely has the means to move about society freely. On the other hand, if the missing person is a child, a rapid emergency response by law enforcement is in order, since a child typically is not at liberty to move about freely for any extended period without being noticed and, furthermore, does not have the legal capacity to decide to run away from home. Considering this, a modern approach to the William Morgan case must then seek to understand who he was and his life circumstances at and leading up to the time of his disappearance in the fall of 1826. Since Morgan was a "senior" adult at the time of his disappearance, his absence would not be considered an emergency; rather, the bio-psycho-social context of his disappearance would need to be taken into account first so as to comprehend whether his departure was voluntary or involuntary. Investigators would need to understand the person and what was going on in his life at the time of his disappearance. As you shall see, that is not an easy question to answer.

Who Was William Morgan?

So, then, investigators would ask, who was William Morgan? According to historical records and writings, William Morgan was born in Culpepper County, Virginia, in 1774 or 1775 to William and Elizabeth Morgan. He became a stonemason and a businessman/merchant in Richmond, and purportedly, he fought in the War of 1812. Dr. Robert Morris, in his detailed presentation of the Morgan case and its aftermath in 1883, cites local attorney Henry Brown's 1830 report, writing that Morgan was a captain in General Andrew Jackson's army and distinguished himself at the Battle of New Orleans.[3] Another assertion about Morgan's early years tying him to the southern conflicts of 1812 refers to him being a member of a pirate band, at times referred to as "Lafitte's gang," according to Stone, who wrote a description of events in 1832. This group of hooligans was said to have been pardoned by President James Madison on the eve of the Battle of New Orleans. Brown added to the story in his 1830 work, stating that Morgan was sentenced to be hanged for this piracy but was pardoned on condition that he would join the army.

It is important to note that Brown, in 1830, clearly states that these war stories about William Morgan were "merely reports, got up and circulated since his abduction, and neither of them are probably entitled to any credit."[4] He goes on to state that if any records existed of Morgan's commission as a captain "as pretended," they would be filed in Washington, D.C., with the War Department. Morris adds in a footnote in his 1883 report that no record nor commissioning paperwork has ever been discovered by the Department of War.[5] More recently, Thomas Knight requested such records from the Department of War and received a letter from the adjutant general relating the following: "No Captain William Morgan has been found as of Virginia Organization in that War [1812]."[6]

So it seems that the "captain" rank and title were based on rumor rather than real service. As we will see, Morgan was not one to shy away from

Left: William Morgan, refined gentleman. *Image license provided by Alamy.com.*

Right: William Morgan, ne'er-do-well. *Image from Dr. Rob Morris, William Morgan, or Political Anti-Masonry (1883).*

misrepresenting himself to advance his opportunities. The title will not be used further in this book since there is no concrete evidence to supports its use and this book takes such evidence as the only reliable and valid basis for scientific decision-making.

After this mysterious period during and after the War of 1812, Morgan married Lucinda Pendleton, daughter of a respected local pastor, in 1819. In 1821, he and his young wife left Virginia and settled in York, Canada (now Toronto), where Morgan tried his hand at brewing. Soon thereafter, misfortune struck, and a fire ruined his brewery, taking away his livelihood and forcing him to move to Rochester, in western New York, where he returned to his original trade of stonemasonry. Eventually, the couple moved to what was then the village of Batavia, around 1824. They had two young children, Lucinda and Thomas "T.J." Jefferson, by the time Morgan disappeared two years later, in 1826.

Reports of Morgan's character were mixed at best. The portraits on this page show the disparate ways that William Morgan was depicted in the nineteenth century. The portrait on the left is a gentlemanly, somewhat scholarly, portrait of William Morgan. Yet alternative descriptions of Morgan deviate dramatically from this formal, learned and demure portrayal. He was known to be frequently out of employment and thus out of funds, fond of drink and predisposed to banter. Morris, in his detailed 1883 volume on the matter, attempts to summarize the known facts about Morgan thus:

> *William Morgan was more than fifty years of age when he was deported from Batavia, New York, in 1826....His constitution was undermined by excesses, intemperance and other vices....He was an idle, worthless fellow....He was unlearned in books and business, scarcely able to read and write.*[7]

The author goes on to cite an anonymous correspondent to support his own less-than-complimentary description:

> *Morgan was the boss crank of his day—a mixture of self-conscious vanity, malice, superstition and excitableness, with a marked ingredient of depravity. Had he possessed a little more sense, he might have been a villain; a little less would have made him a lunatic.*[8]

What Happened to William Morgan in 1826?

After his move to western New York, Morgan apparently was able to join the Royal Arch Masonic Lodge in the neighboring village of Leroy, although to this day, there is no record of his initiatory degree(s), which would have been a prerequisite for him to do so. (Initiatory degrees are the introductory requirements for joining the brotherhood of Freemasons and are documented and archived in the lodge where they occur.) A new Masonic lodge was being founded in Batavia in 1826, and Morgan's application for membership was unofficially denied, as the founding petition document that had borne his signature was seemingly destroyed and a new version made without his signature. (A founding petition document is a petition to the highest lodge in the state, signed by supporting Freemasons, requesting to begin a new lodge.) Needless to say, this upset Morgan, and he soon found alliance with David Miller, the owner of a local print shop and a fellow Batavia resident (as well as a first degree Freemason who had not achieved any higher degrees). Apparently, the two disgruntled Batavians hatched a plan to publish the secret rituals of the Freemasons, motivated by revenge for Morgan's rejection and also for monetary gain. The word got out in this relatively small village that Morgan, Miller and others had the nefarious intent to reveal secrets

Depiction of the kidnapping of William Morgan. *Image license provided by Alamy.com.*

that were, according to oaths taken by first degree Freemasons, not to be shared. It is important to note that when local Freemasons detected that Morgan was lacking any record of his first degree initiation, they realized with consternation and grave concern that since he was not in fact one of them, he was not obliged to secrecy, having taken no oath.

According to news reports from the summer of 1826, Miller's publishing house was set on fire as an initial threat, and then Morgan was harassed until, eventually, he was charged with petty crimes in Canandaigua, New York, and promptly arrested, detained and removed by carriage to Fort Niagara, where he was held in the powder magazine for a number of days.

This is the end of the trail of historical facts whereupon multiple individuals concur and actual courtroom testimony agrees.

At Fort Niagara, a deviation in the narratives begins, so that two possible scenarios develop: (1) Morgan lived on, taken by boat over the Niagara River to Canada, where an agreement had been made earlier with Masonic brothers there to permit him safe passage and a new life (this was an outcome agreed to by Morgan himself), or (2) Morgan met his demise, probably taken by boat to the middle of the Niagara River and dumped overboard and left to drown.

Last known alive location: William Morgan in the powder room of Fort Niagara. *Image license provided by Alamy.com.*

His disappearance caused a major stir in the relatively small town of Batavia. His friend Miller began to raise questions publicly, using his printing press to create a circular. One narrative states that this caused the local Freemasons to consider contacting Morgan by requesting his return via a Native American scout. A second agent was sent after the first scout did not promptly return. The Freemasons recounted that, eventually, the first scout came back with news, and the second soon returned and corroborated the story: Morgan, on reaching the shores of Canada just below Newark, progressed to Hamilton and then York. He remained in the Richmond Hill vicinity for a few days and then moved on to Point Hope. From there, he sold his horse and boarded a lake steamer bound for Boston, Massachusetts. Thus, Morgan was not available for contact and presumably would not return.

With Miller's incendiary printed reports prompting questions from the public, an investigative committee was formed and learned about the arrest and transport of Morgan from Canandaigua to Fort Niagara. The so-called Lewiston Committee reported to the governor of New York and the lieutenant governor of Upper Canada. Rewards were offered by both governments and by private citizens for more information and, of course, for any remains of Morgan. From a modern investigative perspective, Morgan's history—long ago and more recent—suggests that his life had been one clouded in mystery, and in September 1826, at the time of his disappearance, he probably did have reason to want to leave the Batavia vicinity given the rising tensions between himself, Miller and the Masonic brotherhood. This is extremely important contextual information to keep in mind as this investigation into the man's disappearance continues.

Search Efforts

During this time of Morgan's continued absence, and amid the increasing public interest, follow-up search and recovery operations were conducted by law enforcement and volunteers. The Niagara River was repeatedly dragged in search of his body, especially during the fall and even the winter season (weather permitting). Groups of men were reported to have been observed conducting this underwater search procedure along the riverbed. This method of dragging is still used today as a low-technology, low-cost approach to underwater recovery operations in cases where the missing person's precise last known alive location is unknown.

What bystanders would have witnessed in the fall of 1826 was probably quite similar to what is done today. A drag bar (two to six feet long) attached to a boat is dragged along the bottom of the body of water to be searched.

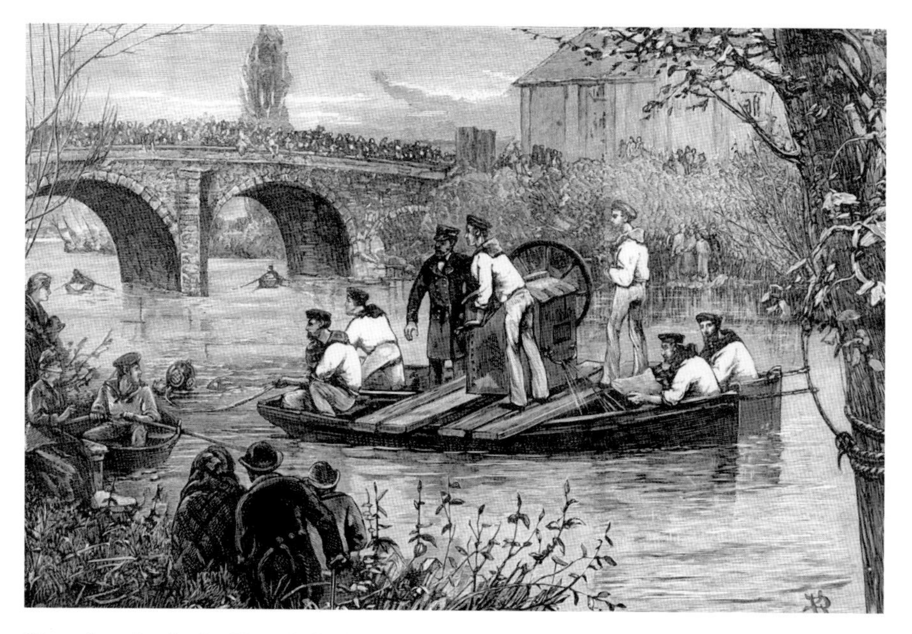

River dragging in the Phoenix Park murder, 1882. *Image license provided by Alamy.com.*

Attached to the drag bar are six- to ten-inch-long chains with flattened barb hooks to snag anything that they encounter, typically clothing in a drowning case. The dragging must be conducted slowly and methodically following a deliberate pattern, oftentimes marked on the surface by buoys. Sweeps overlap so as to ensure full coverage of the designated search area. In the past, cannons or other explosives were used in order to provide a concussion that might jar the body loose from any underwater plants, logs, etc. that might be preventing it from surfacing. This dramatic and morbid procedure is known to have a psychological effect on family members, friends and the general public, especially those in the vicinity of the search. (Morgan's wife, Lucinda, was not reported to be in attendance during any of the searches conducted in 1826–27.) The dramatic process has been used as a gripping and suspenseful element in classic literature, such as Twain's *Huckleberry Finn* and "The Mystery of Marie Rogêt" by Edgar Allen Poe.

When an object is hooked, the forward progress of the boat is stopped immediately, and the object is slowly surfaced by pulling in the lines. This is a time-consuming effort, given that fragile evidence is being handled from a distance and with some force—but hopefully not too much. However, little training is required; thus, volunteers can be enlisted, and much space can be covered.

Along with dragging the Niagara River, men were seen inspecting the shores of Lake Ontario, which receives the Niagara River waters. As with the river-dragging operations, they conducted these shoreline-based investigations during the fall and winter following Morgan's disappearance, but to no avail. Notwithstanding that no body was found, gossip and innuendo gushed like the mighty falls of Niagara, inciting curiosity and intrigue among inhabitants of the Upstate New York region. David Miller continued to contribute willingly to the growing frenzy with the aid of his printing press, paying little attention to the dearth of any concrete evidence.

WHISPERS AND "FISHY" RUMORS

As days, weeks and months passed, imaginations appeared to expand about Morgan's fate. For example, rumors circulated that a sturgeon had washed ashore and its body had been cut open to reveal a pair of boots. The boots were attributed to Morgan! No size nor description was recorded. Investigation deeper into the situation (by Knight in 1950) revealed that no such sturgeon nor boots existed. Furthermore, from a scientific, biological perspective, given the morphology of the benthic, bottom-feeding sturgeon's mouth, it's unlikely that a human body, a boot or a pair of boots would find its way into this particular fish's gut.

Another narrative later determined to be utter fiction involved an "eyewitness" who reported that he had seen a group take Morgan to a field, blindfolded, hands tied. A team of oxen then partially uprooted a large maple tree, Morgan was placed in the cavity and the tree was moved back into position. Other musings that became public speculation involved Morgan being sent over Niagara Falls—or more grisly suggestions, such as Morgan having had his tongue cut out or his throat slit. These and other rumors and hearsay suggestions will be explored in more detail in chapters 4 and 6.

For those who did not understand or disliked the secretive society of the Freemasons, the incident was seen as confirmation of their suspicions. As chapter 3 describes, the hidden nature of some aspects of the Freemasons' activity was interpreted by some as suspect and thereby not trustworthy, even unchristian. Local politicians such as New York state assemblyman and newspaper editor Thurlow Weed of nearby Rochester took hold of the narrative in order to further their own agenda and advance their hold

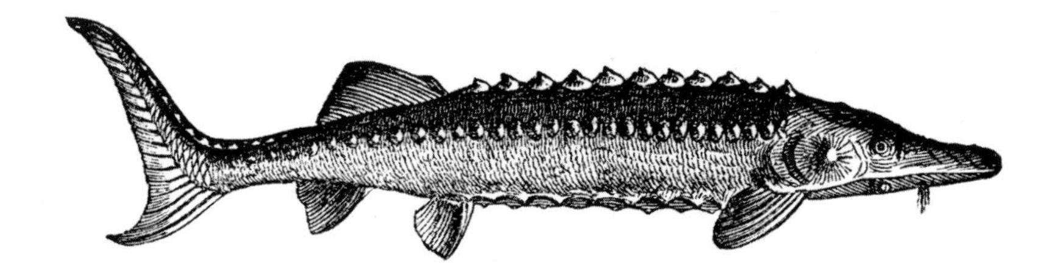

Lake Sturgeon. *Image license provided by Alamy.com.*

on power. To be sure, the Freemasons held much influence in American society as a whole during the early nineteenth century, and those who were not brothers may well have been excluded from the inherent support and connections this fraternal body possessed and exercised for purposes of employment, political endeavors and general community networking. The local non-Masonic politicians were abiding by the guidance of Nicolo Machiavelli, who counseled, "Never waste the opportunity offered by a good crisis." The crisis of Morgan's disappearance and unknown fate, with his wife, Lucinda, and two young children suffering in uncertainty, was the perfect situation on which to focus for political purposes and for those who doubted the Christian purity and even the patriotism of the Freemasons. This political and social division is detailed further in chapters 3 and 6.

Who Was Held Responsible for Morgan's Disappearance?

As the investigations progressed and testimony was documented, four Freemasons became the focus of the Lewiston Committee and then the justice system. They were Nicholas Cheesebro, Edward Sawyer, Loton Lawson and John Sheldon. Trials followed in 1827. Yet without a body, no charge of murder could ever be brought. Those who had purportedly plotted to take Morgan away without his consent—and followed through with that plan—either pleaded guilty to misdemeanor charges (false imprisonment, kidnapping, conspiracy) or were found guilty of and sentenced for the same. Many published accounts of the investigations and trials of these men are available to anyone interested. This book will not delve further into the historically documented crimes that were officially committed, as determined by a jury.

What Were the Political Ramifications of the Morgan Disappearance?

Portrait of Governor Dewitt Clinton of New York. *Image license provided by Alamy.com.*

The political aftermath of this local crime rose from a ripple into a tidal wave of emotion and accusation in the whole of New York State and beyond, into neighboring Pennsylvania and New England as well. An entire political party, aptly named the Anti-Masonic Party, emerged out of the rumors of Morgan's demise. It was a populist movement that played out in Masonic lodges, communities and households, pitting neighbor against neighbor, even kinsman against kinsman. Distrust and suspicion carpeted the atmosphere with a gloom that had not ever been seen by Freemasons in the United States. Membership declined precipitously, lodges were forced to shutter their doors and public shows such as processions were minimized or omitted.

From Miller's local printed agitation and excitement came adroit politicians' speeches and city newspaper entries, from Thurlow Weed even to the better-known national figures William Henry Seward and Martin Van Buren. They used this suspicious event to further their own interests in the state governorship, which at the time was held by the talented Dewitt Clinton, who just happened to be a very prominent leader of the New York Freemasons and a potential candidate for president of the United States. Even the current U.S. president, John Quincy Adams, saw Clinton as a potential threat.

Over a year after the disappearance of Morgan and months after the trials of those who conspired to move him to Niagara had concluded, a renewed excitement arose from the shores of Lake Ontario in the town of Carlton, in Orleans County. A body had finally emerged from those dark waters.

Chapter 2

IDENTIFICATION ALCHEMY

Coroners' Inquests

Quis custódiat ipsos custodes?
Who is watching the watchman?
—Latin maxim

The Slater Inquest

Indeed, the body of a man had been discovered on the banks of Lake Ontario at the mouth of Oak Orchard Creek in Orleans County on October 7, 1827.

According to local residents, carrion birds had drawn the attention of early-rising passersby, who noticed the body and called the local coroner, Giles Slater (as reported by Mock in 1930). Slater arrived quickly, and twenty-four people were assembled as his jury. Some of them assisted in getting the body out of the water, putting it on a shutter that had come from a nearby barn and taking it up the bank. Morris noted in his 1883 account that the body was "heavier than they had supposed" and "more than one…turned aside to discharge the contents of his stomach. Even the official succumbed to the awful disgust."[9]

To remedy this natural repulsion, a "jug of spirits was brought…[and] under alcoholic influence the work of inspection was performed."[10] Findings were nevertheless generated, with the results of this initial investigation listing the following biological characteristics as reported verbatim:

Length: 5'10" (70 inches)
No scars
Age: Approximately 46 years
Heavy whiskers
Thick hair
Teeth sound—nothing remarkable
Personal effects included:
clothing—described
religious tracts in one of the pockets

It was recorded that a "two-foot rule" was used for the body length measurement (also known as "stature" by forensic practitioners/medical doctors). This was the most common measuring tool used by woodworkers in the nineteenth century and was also known as the "two-foot folding rule."

There was some witness commentary on the length measurement being slightly inaccurate due to either the rule being slightly "off" from the base of the feet or from the body's somewhat bent posture in death. It seems five feet, ten inches would have been the minimal body length measurement, with witnesses noting that the deceased, if not bent in death, would have stretched out to a full stature taller than this stated height.

In addition, anecdotal commentary from two of the witnesses (and inquest jurors) was as follows, as reported by Morris in 1883: "The two Potters who first discovered the body knew William Morgan....[This body bore] no likeness."[11]

So that the reader understands what was occurring here, a coroner's inquest was a local investigative process used in countries following common law (i.e., the United Kingdom and the United States) that sought to answer the questions of manner and cause of death, conducted by a coroner with a court reporter and at least six jurors present. The jurors were to be citizens of the county in which the death occurred. Thus, the goal was to determine a verdict on the manner and cause of death. *Manner of death* falls into one of five categories, still used today on death certificates: homicide, suicide, accidental, natural or undetermined. *Cause of death* is the medical explanation for the death: for example, cardiac arrest, suffocation, etc.

The verdict in Giles Slater's inquest on the banks of Lake Ontario that day was rendered: "found drowned." Clearly this report provided only the cause of death and did not respond to the manner.

The clothes of the unidentified male were dried and placed in the hands of the magistrate in the Town of Carlton. A coffin was procured and the body shrouded and, by order of the coroner, buried in situ. Following these

Point Breeze, Town of Carlton, today. *Photograph by Steven R. Bunch.*

Two-foot rule. *Image license provided by Alamy.com.*

actions, as usual, the report of the coroner's inquest was published in local papers. This was a way to obtain possible identification of the victim from those who were missing kin, friends, acquaintances or coworkers.

The announcement of an unidentified middle-aged male body in the area most certainly aroused public attention. Those who had not achieved justice for Morgan's disappearance and suspected murder were quick to react. Thurlow Weed and an entourage headed to Carlton on October 13, where the body was disinterred from its original burial location and brought to the Town of Carlton office. Witnesses observed that at that point, "all human identity had gone," according to Mock in his 1930 report.[12]

This description reinforces the well-adhered-to maxim of investigators: time is one's enemy, and the closer one is to the event being investigated, the better the information. For example, res gestae ("things done") witness statements (that is, those made immediately following an incident) are still looked on by investigators as the most valid and accurate statements that can be obtained, since they are natural, spontaneous and occur without deliberation. In the case of decomposing remains, any assessment will be greatly affected by even the slightest passage of time.

Despite the diminished quality of the human remains under investigation, these Rochester-based inquirers desired to perform their own investigation, which resulted in a second official coroner's inquest on October 15, 1827. According to reports, between October 13, which was a Saturday, and October 15, a Monday, the body was guarded for two days by Weed's appointees. On October 15, Lucinda Morgan and other friends and acquaintances of William Morgan, as well as compatriots of Weed, were brought to Carlton to participate.

THE BROWN INQUEST

Another Orleans County coroner (each county had three), Robert M. Brown, headed this second inquest. There were twenty-four jurymen assembled at this time. (It is not clear whether this jury was in compliance with the law—i.e., all jurors were citizens of the county in which the death occurred—or, rather, if some from Genesee County were included.) The body was "black, bloated, putrid, and offensive beyond anything conceivable" according to Morris in 1883.[13] Interestingly, the head was reported as being "nearly bald" now, and a "bunch of whiskers" had somehow disappeared. The decedent's "ears and nostrils" were now seen to be "adorned with long, white hairs."[14]

Lucinda Morgan provided officials in attendance with a detailed description of her husband before any physical investigation process on that day began. She and others supplied the following biological characteristics:

Height: 5'6" (66 inches)
Scar on one toe from surgery due to frostbite
Age: approximately 50 years
No whiskers
Bald
Teeth: double "clear round"

Double teeth may require some explanation, since this is not a term familiar to most; these are conjoined teeth that have been described by dentists using a variety of terms, such as *gemination*, *fusion* or *twinning*, according to a 2007 article by Méndez, Junquera and Gallego. The etiology of these typically asymptomatic dental conditions—since all these terms apply to different anomalies of the teeth—is not known; however, suggestions include environmental factors, trauma, systemic diseases, vitamin deficiencies or genetic predisposition, according to Méndez, Junquera and Gallego's 2007 study. Tooth fusion and gemination—that is, "double teeth"—are rare, according to Wellbury, Duggal and Hosey's 2019 research. Studies of White populations show that in the permanent dentition (adult teeth), the prevalence is low: between 0.1 percent and 0.2 percent. Bilateral double teeth are even more uncommon, with a prevalence of .02 percent. (In other words, among every ten thousand people in a given population, two would present this trait.) It seems as though Morgan had the latter, even more rare, dental condition, with the "clear round" indicating teeth were conjoined in the front and back of his jaws. This rare condition would make a dental identification relatively easy to accomplish if William Morgan's remains were in fact discovered.

It should be noted that no measurements were taken at this particular inquest. However, those who knew Morgan were, one by one, forced to glance at the decomposing mass and "identify" the body, giving sworn statements. Mrs. Morgan, when induced to view the remains, "turned hastily away from the pile of carrion" to sign a sworn statement that she was "fully convinced in her mind that it was her husband" according to Morris's 1883 account.[15]

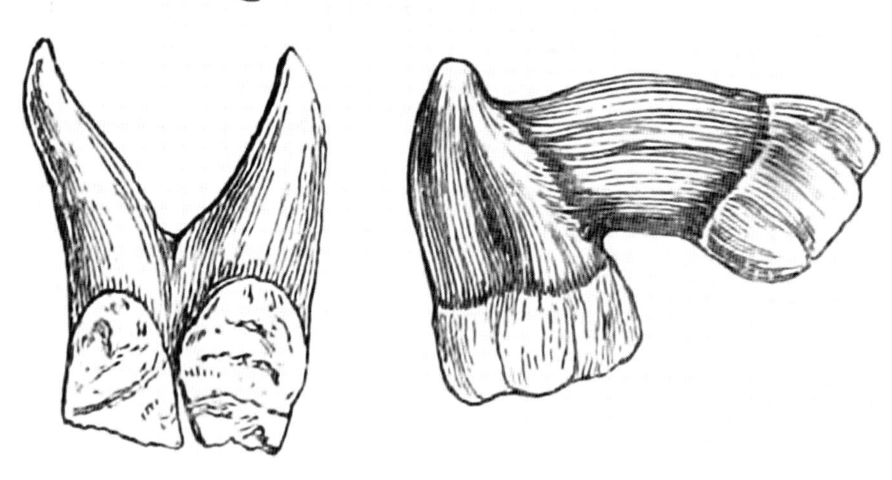

Dental pathology diagram, with dental gemination shown. *Image license provided by Alamy.com.*

Yet a problem presented itself with the personal effects—i.e., the clothing and the religious tracts found on the decedent. In reference to these items, Lucinda reportedly stated, "I can recognize no part of it [the clothing] as the same as which my husband had on when he went away, nor the tract." About the handwriting, she stated, "I cannot swear to though one of the two letters somewhat resemble his," as reported by Morris in 1883. Despite the inconsistencies, she still was "fully convinced" that this was her husband.

How could this be? In modern-day death investigations, this process, called *visual identification*, is still relied on; however, the risks involved in obtaining a false positive or a false negative identification are better known and have been documented in the literature.

Corder and Sribanditmongkol, in a 2006 book, summarize that visual recognition of cadavers or their photographs by kin or acquaintances is the simplest form of identification but is prone to errors. Therefore, whenever possible, death investigators recommend that it should be complemented (verified) by other means of forensic identification. The traumatic nature of the next of kin viewing their expired loved one may result in a rushed or inaccurate assessment of the remains. In addition, due to the decomposition process, traumatic injury or a combination of the two, the remains may have little to no similarity to the appearance of the person when he or she lived. Furthermore, in Lucinda Morgan's situation, there was great pressure at the time, given the context of distrust and political strife, for her to conclude that this was in fact her husband—not to mention the groupthink of the company she kept at the time of the second inquest. All these factors should be considered in an attempt to understand Lucinda Morgan's official statement.

Others familiar with Morgan "testified that they had seen such resemblances and marks of identification in the decomposed human mass" as to be so certain, according to Mock's 1930 report.[16] Interestingly, Thurlow Weed did not make such a strong statement. He stated that he did not know Morgan personally, yet,

> *Mr. Fitch had told him that Morgan's ears were full of long white hairs. So he examined the said ears very carefully and found several hairs in them, long and white, which* came out upon touching them. *Furthermore, he found a large number of said hairs* deposited in a mass in the bottom of the ear [emphasis mine].

These hairs supposedly corresponded to the description "previously had," according to Morris's 1883 report. Palmer, in 1946, also wrote of the "peculiar long white hairs in his [Morgan's] ears and nostrils."[17] Why were these not observed and discussed in the first inquest? Also, hairs coming out "upon touching them" and "deposited in a mass" sound more like unnatural,

Making a "visual" identification: extremely difficult for family members yet still done today. *Image license provided by Alamy.com.*

out-of-context associations. We will discuss these peculiar "ear hairs" later in this chapter.

Two medical authorities were included in this jury, Dr. Ezra Strong (a dentist) and Dr. John Henry. Strong had apparently pulled two of Morgan's teeth antemortem, and Lucinda Morgan had kept those teeth and brought them with her to the inquest. The report stated that Dr. Strong "put them in this mouth, and they *just about fill* the vacancy," according to Morris in 1883 (emphasis mine).[18] Dr. Henry had treated Morgan when he lived in Rochester and was "*unwilling to say whether this is Morgan's body or not*, though teeth, head and hair resemble his," again according to Morris's 1883 report (emphasis mine).[19]

Notwithstanding the imperfection of the dental reconstruction that was attempted by Dr. Strong and the clear uncertainty of Dr. Henry, the verdict of this second inquest of "twenty-three good and lawful men" was that this was William Morgan and he had died "by suffocation by drowning," as summarized by Morris 1883.[20] Again, cause of death is stated, yet manner is not.

It should be highlighted here—as something undoubtedly more than an afterthought—that this second coroner's inquest may have also been a reaction to the doubts about the original inquest that occurred a few days prior, since land records show that Giles Slater, the original coroner, was in fact a Freemason. In *Landmarks of Orleans County, New York*, a record dating to 1894, Giles Slater's signature appears on a petition for a lodge to be established in the Town of Ridgeway (adjacent to the Town of Carlton) in 1815. Was it thought that Freemasons might have misrepresented the identification of the body? Coroner Brown was not listed in any record as a Freemason.

The body, now officially "identified" as that of William Morgan, was moved ceremoniously to Batavia on October 19, 1827. David Miller did not hesitate to give prior notice with the use of "thousands of dodgers" providing news that "Morgan's Body Is Found," according to Knight's 1950 retelling.[21] Crowds gathered to see the procession, and "funeral orations… poured forth," according to Mock's 1930 report.[22] The decomposing corpse was buried, this time in Batavia, but not before it was displayed on a James Brisbane's lawn, located in the village center. Knight relays that "many thousands of people suffered the stench in order to participate in this strangest of all funeral spectacles."[23]

In the meantime, far away in what was then Upper Canada, a Mrs. Sarah Munro became aware of the news of the body found on the lakeshore and traveled with her son and a family friend to check if the body was that of her missing husband, Timothy. Mr. Munro had departed their home not long ago, on September 24, 1827, by boat and had not returned. Sarah met with Bates Cook and others of the aforementioned Lewiston Committee to describe her husband and possibly connect him to the remains now buried in Batavia.

The Hurlburt Inquest

Sarah Munro described her husband's clothing in minute detail, mentioning alterations that she herself had made to the pantaloons, according to Morris's 1883 account.[24] Other physical characteristics that she mentioned seemed definitively consistent with the remains, so a third coroner's inquest jury was empaneled in Batavia on October 29, 1827. The body was again disinterred, and twenty-four jurors were assembled. One of the coroners of Genesee County, Jonathan Hurlburt, presided. Sarah Munro testified, as did her son, David, and their family friend John Cross. The latter had seen Timothy Munro on the day he was last known to be alive and noted that Munro's clothing and religious tracts were consistent with this discovered person's personal effects.

Dr. H. Vinton noted that he "started" the head hair (meaning that he caused it to work loose from its place or fastening) from the forehead and was therefore "certain it grew there," according to Morris's 1883 report.[25] The reader is reminded that during the second inquest, in contrast, the unique white hairs in the ears were "pulled out" with a mere touch and likewise were "collected in a mass," indicating an unnatural means of deposition.

Notably, measurements were taken during this third inquiry, as they were during the first. Body measurements were obtained resulting in a length of 69.5 inches (5 feet, 9.5 inches), but it was noted (again) that the body was in a bent position, resulting in an underestimate of what would have been the actual measurement by one to two inches. Thomas McCully testified with regard to the stature, since he was similar in height to Morgan and reported that he was often mistaken for him when approached from behind. McCully was 65 inches (5 feet, 5 inches) tall and weighed about 135 pounds. Russell Dyer concurred with this.

Additional medical experts testified in this third inquest, including Dr. Hall, who had been part of the first inquest. He commented that the hair

Coroner's inquest. *Image license provided by Alamy.com.*

on the head was "thick" and "covered [the] forehead and continued back" (again according to Morris).[26] The teeth were described as a "good set," but no mention was made of them being "double." Five were said to be missing, yet it is not clear if these were missing post mortem or antemortem. "Some whiskers" were observed as well by Dr. Hall. Moses Wood, Daniel English and the "two Potters" who had been at the first inquest corroborated Hall's recollections.

Dr. John Cates Jr., a surgeon and practitioner from Batavia, also offered medical expert testimony about the "scraped toe" of Morgan. Cates "cut open the feet, but there was no indication" that any of them had been surgically affected. The reader will remember that Lucinda had reported to the second inquest jury in her list of biological traits that her husband had had surgery on his left big toe when it was affected by frostbite. The physician had had to cut open the flesh and scrape the bone, a procedure known as *debridement*, where dead, devitalized, contaminated tissue or foreign material is surgically excised from a wound. In cases of frostbite, the proximity of the surgeon's scalpel to bone depends on the degree of frostbite (e.g., second degree leads to blisters, which are far more superficial than fourth degree, which presents blackened, necrotic tissue where scraping down to bone may be required). Such scraping, with a less-than-careful surgeon or severe tissue damage, could leave marks on the bone. It is interesting that Dr. Henry of the second inquest had not made any observations in this regard—nor apparently even attempted to do so—even though Lucinda had mentioned the prior trauma.

Dr. Cates was the first and only expert to opine on the postmortem interval (PMI), otherwise known as "time since death," stating that the body was "only in the first stage of decomposition" and that it "could not have been dead over two months at the furthest," according to Morris's report.[27] According to Cates, there was

> *no cleaving of the flesh from the bones or tendons; the flesh adheres to the bone; stomach is in perfect state and has the same tenacity as that of a person recently dead.*[28]

Given the highly precise descriptions given by Sarah Munro and her accompanying party, as well as the more invasive and detailed medical inquiry and testimony from Drs. Vinton and Cates, the verdict of this third inquest was that the remains were identified as those of Timothy Munro. Both the cause and manner of death were determined:

> [He] *came to his death by drowning…that in crossing the Niagara River from Fort May area to Fort George in a skiff the same upset in the said River by means whereupon the said Timothy Munro became* accidentally drowned *to wit on the 26th Day of September 1827* [emphasis mine].

This date was near to the day that Munro had departed by boat from Newcastle for Newark or Fort George. As stated, in this, the third and final inquest, both cause and manner of death were provided. Thirteen jurors signed the verdict. Science was referenced as having led this final inquest to the right and final determination. The description of what occurred does show that the most intrusive and in-depth analysis was performed during this final inquiry. And thus the remains of Mr. Timothy Munro were once again moved, this time to their final and rightful resting place in Upper Canada.

THE DISTURBING SERIES OF inquests and the case of temporary "mistaken" identity resulted in questions from the public regarding how this could have occurred. How could the remains of the lost Canadian have been confused with Morgan's? Was there a calculation rather than an honest mistake in this? Details trickled out to curious citizens of western New York, and rumors began to emerge pointing to an insidious political plot on the part of Weed and his coterie.

Remember that during the second inquest, the corpse—after being disinterred from its original burial location and transported to Carlton—was reportedly "nearly bald," with the whiskers much reduced, and white hairs had, this time, somehow been noticed growing from Morgan's ears. The reader is also reminded here that two days passed between the deposition of the remains in Carlton on Saturday, October 13, and the second inquest on Monday, October 15, that followed, during which Thurlow Weed had the body guarded so as to prevent any reaction from suspected Freemasons. Yet the transformation that had occurred between the Slater inquest and the Brown inquest cannot be attributed to any natural decomposition process. Hairs do not move from crown to head orifices passively. Thus, the question arises that trained investigators must ask: *Quis custodiat ipsos custodes?* Who was watching the watchman? Could Weed's "guards" be trusted?

Many of the rumors implicated Weed, the newsman and political boss, of "having the bearded corpse shaved, and the hairs plucked from the forehead and thrust into the ears and nostrils," according to Palmer's 1946 report.[29] Weed, when confronted with this accusation, reportedly stated that the remains "were a good enough Morgan until after the election" (as quoted by Palmer in 1946).[30] Weed denied having said this repeatedly thereafter. Even on his deathbed, he distanced himself completely from having had any involvement in disfiguring Timothy Munro's corpse in a published, formal, notarized statement.

The details of the three coroners' inquests are provided from sources that date to the nineteenth century (e.g., Morris's historical account) and actual court records (e.g., the Genesee County report on the third inquest). These are treated here as our best res gestae statements—those official statements made close to the time of the events. Yet it should be observed here that alternative narratives of the death investigation involving the corpse ultimately identified as that of Timothy Munro exist and can be found on the internet. For example, a website that purports to be the "Premier Website for Early Mormon History" (see bibliography for further details) provides a commingled account of inquest no. 1 and inquest no. 2, stating that Brown was the coroner for inquest no. 1 on October 7, 1827 (and omitting any mention of Slater). In addition, an erroneous reference to "double-teeth," the conflation of Batavia residents with Carlton residents and a haphazard presentation of the processes indicate a lack of attention to proximate historical sources and a careless, inaccurate presentation of events following the discovery Munro's body. The reader should not fail to note that the website is not focused on Masonic history but rather on Mormon history, thus offering, openly and publicly, its bias. We will see in the following chapter and other pages that particular Christian sects—not only that of the Mormon faith—have had problems with Freemasons and have had no qualms about making their concerns known.

The final chapter of this book follows up on themes such as this particular example of the commingling of separate historical events. Recommendations for how a reader today can carefully assess such narrative accounts are offered.

Chapter 3

WHAT FORCE DENIES THE SENSES?

An error does not become truth by reason of multiplied propagation, nor does truth become error because nobody sees it.
—Mahatma Gandhi

As the reader has seen, the first and third inquests used the scientific process of making methodical and systematic observations and delivered the jury verdict that the remains found in Orleans County were not those of William Morgan. The second inquest did not use any measurements and relied on nonscientific identification processes—e.g., visual identification, hearsay reports from acquaintances—and determined that the remains were those of Morgan. In this second inquest, even Morgan's own wife reported that the decomposing mass had been her husband in life.

The question must be asked, then: What force or forces were at work at this time in the United States and specifically western New York State to deny, confound and/or obfuscate (purposefully or not) the observational senses of numerous individuals involved in the second inquest to identify—in a formal, medico-legal setting—a body as Morgan's that had numerous physical indicators inconsistent with the missing man from Batavia?

Common sense informs us that political machinations were influential in arranging for a second inquest and potentially pressuring witnesses to conclude that Munro's body was Morgan's. If the account of Weed making a statement about "a good enough Morgan" was accurate, then a misidentification was seen by him as a useful tool, politically, for even a short period. We must then explore the political atmosphere of Batavia and beyond to come to an understanding of how human senses can be turned off, willingly or not, even momentarily.

According to Palmer's 1946 account, New York State was in political disarray in the early nineteenth century—essentially in a power vacuum—owing in part to the loss of Founding Father and highly respected New Yorker Alexander Hamilton. In 1804, Hamilton died in a legal duel with Vice President Aaron Burr. The Federalist Party, to which Hamilton belonged, "felt his loss keenly."[31] The need for direction and a strong leader to fill his shoes was clear. The new generation of politicians was divided, seeking a path into the new century in a country still in its infancy.

That direction, for some, took a reactionary form, in opposition to the efforts of the New York State government to build the Erie Canal. As mentioned earlier, Governor Dewitt Clinton, a powerful, well-respected Freemason and skilled politician, was clearly for the canal—hence its nickname, Clinton's Ditch. The so-called Bucktails, aligned with Martin Van Buren, were opposed to the effort. When, in 1826, Van Buren aligned with Clinton and agreed that the canal was in the best interests of the state, his followers were again unmoored.

In addition to the regional disagreements on the need for the Erie Canal, inhabitants of Batavia and surrounding Genesee County had other concerns that may have influenced their political stances and choices. Historian Robert Silsby, in 1961, wrote that resentment of the Holland Land Company (HLC) among the early settlers there was growing at this time. The HLC had begun land sales in the area in 1801, under the leadership of Joseph Ellicott. Yet some recipients were unable or unwilling to complete their down payments, and fears emerged that the HLC would take action against those who were unable to or refused to keep up with their payments. Further complaints regarding high land prices and low community project assistance were also on the rise after 1819, according to Silsby.

Enter Thurlow Weed. Then a twenty-nine-year-old editor of the *Rochester Telegraph*, veteran of the War of 1812 and former member of the New York State Assembly, Weed was an adroit political operator who appeared to work most effectively behind the scenes to accomplish political goals rather than in the forefront as an officeholder. Access to and control of the *Rochester Telegraph* further enhanced his effectiveness in steering local and state narratives and affecting public opinion (and thus the collective consciousness).

Weed's political instincts must have been piqued in 1826 when he encountered the local outrage and curiosity regarding Morgan's disappearance. The underlying anti-Masonic sentiment was palpable. An additional motivating issue against which a group of people could react had been found. Weed kept the public "informed" by means of the printing press. Locally, Miller's flyers and dodgers filled in the details. As we have seen, Weed orchestrated a second coroner's inquest that led to the misidentification of Timothy Munro's remains. Soon he formed the Anti-Masonic Party, the first third political party in the United States, and moved to Albany to print a new paper titled the *Anti-Masonic Enquirer.* New York City followed suit in 1827 with the *National Observer.*

Thurlow Weed, New York State assemblyman and newspaper editor. *Image license provided by Alamy.com.*

There was clearly a need for a focal point for public reaction after the Erie Canal gained consensus in the state's power hubs. But from where did the dramatic public reaction to the seemingly well-to-do and honorable Freemasons emerge? As Morris, in 1883, stated,

> *Amidst the prosperity…there were elements of opposition; there were causes working; coals upon which it only needed that popular breath be blown to kindle into flame.*[32]

Beneath the surface of society simmered a sense among some of jealousy, perhaps? Disgruntlement? Something else? As with residents' complaints and concerns about the HLC, the sense of "haves" and "have-nots" may have been growing among the local population. Morris, in 1883, listed a number of reasons why there may have been these "elements of opposition" to the Freemasons at this time, which are paraphrased in the following paragraphs.

Other important and well-known politicians besides the more locally known Thurlow Weed may have resented the Freemasons as a result of being rejected. The example given by Morris is that of Thaddeus Stevens of Pennsylvania, a well-known member of the United States House of Representatives and ardent advocate for abolition. Apparently

Representative Stevens had, at some point in his life, applied for initiation to a Masonic lodge only to be blackballed due to a "physical defect."[33] Stevens was known to walk with a limp since he was born with a clubfoot, a condition where one or both feet are rotated inward and downward, at times resulting in the affected foot and leg being smaller in size than the opposite side. Morris surmised that Weed, too, may have had his application for initiation rejected, yet no record of that has been discovered.

In addition to prominent public figures feeling a sense of resentment or indignation at being rejected by this fraternal order, those who had a relative (a son, father or brother) who suffered the same perceived insult might also harbor similar feelings. In addition, any man who had been expelled from a lodge for un-Masonic conduct might bear a grudge against those who judged him. Demitted Masons (those who had left the lodge of their own free will for one reason or another) also could harbor festering negative sentiments against the order.

A different group that may have "blown" the "popular breath" in order to "kindle the flame" was opportunists, such as politicians who "sniffed the battle afar off" and anticipated spoils and plunder. In this group would also be those involved in newspaper publication, "seeking for an unworn hobby," as relayed by Morris in 1883.[34] News media at the time were in a phase of openness about political affiliation, according to Mark Levin's 2019 book *Unfreedom of the Press*. Their biases in the political world were known and even promoted; thus, readers of newspapers and magazines at the time were well aware that a sort of partisanship was being presented in the pages.

Thaddeus Stevens, U.S. representative from Pennsylvania. *Image license provided by Alamy.com.*

Less obvious sources of negative opinions regarding Freemasons could be found among different religious groups. Members of various worship communities historically held the Freemasons in suspicion. Members of the Roman Catholic Church, for example, learned that societies founded on "liberty of conscience" were to be despised. Likewise, Protestant fanatics thought that the only fraternities that needed to exist in a Christian country were Christian ones. Although Freemasonry utilizes the Bible in its rituals, it does not require Christian faith of its members. For staunch Protestants, this worked against them. For deists and atheists, given their beliefs or lack thereof, the opposite was true. These alternative believers or nonbelievers might easily have reacted negatively to a body that centered its rituals around the Bible during its processions and public and private rituals.

In addition to this list of groups that might have held some anti-Masonic views, Morris, in 1883, blamed Freemason leadership for some of the negative feelings in society. He suggested that leaders had "widened the door" to allow some in who should not have been. Some who were initiated were "affiliated in Masonry…not assimilated."[35] On the other side of the coin was the fact that many applications were being received for initiation during this time of prosperity, and thus, the lodges were able to be more selective with those whom they permitted to join. Necessarily then, there were more rejected and thus more out in society with a reason to harbor resentment. As Morris summarizes, the rejection turned to revenge, which turned to hatred.[36]

On a broader, national scale, another source of distrust at this particular point in time may have been the recent visit paid to the United States by the Marquis de Lafayette in 1824–25. Lafayette was the last surviving French general of the Revolutionary War and received a hero's welcome on his twenty-four-state tour. President James Monroe had invited the famous general to celebrate the upcoming fiftieth anniversary of the young country, as well as inspire the next generation of Americans.

The Freemasons were part of this public outpouring of honor and respect since, according to Lafayette's own writings, he became a Freemason after meeting George Washington. It is said that he was initiated during the winter of 1777–78, and it is believed that Washington himself acted as Master of the Lodge during the ceremony. Dr. George W. Chaytor stated during an address given at Lafayette Lodge No. 14 in Wilmington, Delaware, on January 18, 1875:

> *He* [Lafayette] *was not a Mason when he landed in America.…The Army under Washington, in December 1777, retired to Valley Forge, where they wintered. Connected to the Army was a Lodge. It was at Valley Forge that he was made a Mason.*[37]

The pomp and circumstance that accompanied Lafayette's visit may have caused concern and raised questions among any with remaining Loyalist sentiments about Freemasons' allegiance overseas.

The Freemasons were well respected and upstanding members of society, yet they did have "enemies" among the populace. "Public opposition…needs

General Lafayette. *Image license provided by Alamy.com.*

only a bugle call, a rallying cry, to organize such persons into an army of offense" according to Morris in 1883.[38] It seems the people were ready for Morgan, or even a "good enough Morgan," at this time.

It is important to note that today, there still exists much misunderstanding about Freemasonry. A 2022 publication by the History Channel focused on secret societies begins its chapter on Freemasons with the question: "An ominous secret society with bizarre rites—or a fraternal order of do-gooders dedicated to brotherly love and philanthropy?"[39]

As earlier stated, anti-Freemason sentiment was so strong that the country's first third political party emerged: the Anti-Masonic Party. It began as a single-issue party, completely focused on opposition to Freemasonry. Eventually it expanded its platform as it moved from being a state party in New York to a major national party. In New York, its immediate local leaders were, of course, Thurlow Weed, along with Solomon Southwick and William Wirt. Other more nationally prominent New York politicians who added their articulate voices to the Anti-Masonic cause were William Seward and Millard Fillmore. The popular acclaim and adept political skills of these leaders drove the Anti-Masons into an important position at the time, constituting an alternative to Andrew Jackson's Democrats and John Quincy Adams's National Republicans.

NYS Position/Party	**1820**	**1830**	**1835**
State Senator			
Dem-Rep Bucktail	19	0	N/A
Dem-Rep Clintonian	13	0	N/A
Jacksonian	N/A	23	N/A
National Republican	N/A	3	N/A
Anti-Mason	N/A	6	0
Democrat	N/A	N/A	28
Whig	N/A	N/A	4

NYS Position/Party	1820	1830	1835
State Assembly			
Dem-Rep Bucktail	42	0	N/A
Dem-Rep Clintonian	9	0	N/A
Federalist	19	0	N/A
Jacksonian	N/A	87	N/A
National Republican	N/A	3	N/A
Anti-Mason	N/A	25	0
Workingmen	N/A	1	0
Democrat	N/A	N/A	94
Whig	N/A	N/A	33
Unaffiliated/Unreported	51	12	0

Table of New York political affiliation before and after the Morgan affair. *Based on Jabez D. Hammond, 1852, and Franklin B. Hough, 1858.*

The movement after the disappearance of Morgan began with town halls that spread anti-Masonic sentiment—resentment?—beyond the borders of the western New York counties where it all began. Newspapers helped continue the dissemination of information. This negative sentiment moved from these local gatherings to the New York State legislature. The Anti-Masonic Party was established in the state in 1827, and the election that took place that year surprised everyone. Palmer, in 1954, wrote that the party's "success astonished even the Anti-Masons themselves and opened the eyes of the politicians to the fact that the new party was a force to be reckoned with."[40] Anyone arguing that "only one" case of anything is not enough to cause concern or warrant attention need only study the case of Morgan to give him- or herself pause. Economist Nassim Taleb, in 2007, used the metaphor of the black swan to describe such events: that is, extremely rare and unpredictable events, beyond typical expectations, that may have severe consequences. For Freemasons, Morgan's disappearance was one such event; the impact it had on U.S. political history and the course that our country took almost two hundred years ago cannot be denied.

To show the success that this third party had: in 1833, the Anti-Masonic contingent outnumbered the National Republicans in the New York State legislature. Presidential candidate Jackson took note of this party with caution and made conciliatory gestures. (Importantly, Jackson was a very prominent Mason from North Carolina.) John Quincy Adams, who would run for a second term, pronounced formally in the *Albany Daily Advertiser* in April 1828 that he was not a Mason and never would be. Weed and others fanned the flames since they supported Adams.

Year	**Anti-Masonic Party Reps**	**Total Reps**
1828	5	213
1830	17	213
1832	25	240
1834	16	242
1836	7	242
1838	6	242

Anti-Masonic Party affiliation in the U.S. House of Representatives from 1828 to 1838. *Based on Formisano, 2010, and Formisano and Kutolowski, 1977.*

The radical faction of the Anti-Masonic Party wanted Freemasonry eradicated and would not work with other National Republican nominees for public office, such as New York governor. Their inability to seek a middle ground eventually caused much concern among those looking for harmony, and their intransigence divided the right-wing vote so that Democrat candidates reaped the benefits. However, as stated earlier, the Anti-Masonic Party did take on an expanded platform as it became a national party, centering on internal improvements and protective tariffs. Pennsylvania, Vermont and Maine were also affected by the Anti-Masonic Party and the broader anti-Masonic movement.

However, by 1838, the party had expended all its political currency, and by 1840 its members had, for the most part, merged into the new Whig Party. (As a historical note, Weed's involvement in anti-Masonic political campaigns did not die with the party of that name. He was a campaign advisor for Zachary Taylor in 1848 when Taylor ran against Lewis Cass, a senator from Michigan and cofounder of the Grand Lodge of Michigan Freemasons.)

Yet the damage to the Freemasons had been done. The formation of a third party and the elections that followed during the ensuing decade (1826–36) demonstrated the power of the anti-Masonic sentiment among the people. The ranks of the Freemasons also reflected what a negative impact this public response to the Morgan affair and the official embodiment of it in the Anti-Masonic Party had on lodges in the northeastern United States. Membership declined, meetings were cancelled, public events and showings were minimized, brothers demitted in order to avoid retribution, lodges were shuttered and some closed permanently. There was a very real price to pay if one was a Freemason.

Historical records show the diminution in lodges and membership following the "Morgan Affair." For example, five hundred lodges existed in New York State, with 20,000 members, in 1829; in 1832, there were only fifty-two lodges with 1,500 members, according to Morris in 1883. A dramatic reduction indeed—more than a 90 percent decrease—based initially on rumors and innuendo bubbling up in a small upstate village. Lodge membership over time did recover; however, this rejuvenation took decades. And as the ranks of Freemasons declined, in the years that immediately followed this mysterious man's disappearance, a number of opportunities to name Morgan's killer presented themselves in the form of confessors to the murder or to the conspiracy to commit this heinous act.

Chapter 4

CONFESSIONS TO THE "MURDER" OF MORGAN

Secrecy sets barriers between men, but at the same time offers the seductive temptation to break through the barriers by gossip or confession.
—George Simmel

With a new and empowered anti-Masonic faction on the rise, the tide of "haves" and "have-nots" had turned in Upstate New York and the country as a whole. Such moments provide opportunities for those who might have been, or at least felt, disenfranchised in the foregoing time. A new popular viewpoint emerged post-1827, with all its political and societal implications.

Since this book takes an investigative/scientific perspective, focusing on evidence whenever possible, we cannot ignore that, within this new sociopolitical context, individuals did in fact come forward and confess to the crime of murdering William Morgan. All but one confession came from individuals whose soundness of mind was never questioned at the time. Other aspects of their character may have been in doubt, that is to be sure. The various confessors are detailed here, and their possible reasons for confessing are also addressed.

The admission of a man going by R.H. HILL came not long after Morgan's disappearance had garnered much attention. He came forward voluntarily in Buffalo, New York, sometime before 1832, and admitted to killing Morgan.[41] In jail, he wrote a statement summarizing his claim. He admitted to the murder because, he explained, his conscience weighed heavy owing to his

Making a confession to law enforcement. *Image license provided by Alamy.com.*

participation as the principal in killing a man he had never seen before. He did not name his accomplices, since he was supposedly bound by oath with them not to do so. He was transferred to Niagara County, where the crime was said to have occurred, and jailed anew in Lockport.

Before a grand jury, he repeated his confession; however, his narrative had no supporting evidence or any corroboration from another party and was thus discredited. Hill was discharged since he was considered to be afflicted with a diseased mind, according to Knight in 1950.[42]

MR. THOMAS HAMILTON had been expelled from Masonry and thus did not have an objective opinion on the Morgan matter. He took hold of the opportunity provided by the Morgan disappearance to lecture from town to town on Masonry and its secret handshakes and signs—and, in addition, openly charged that Morgan had been murdered, providing much detail on how it was done, again according to Knight in 1950.[43] Hamilton was fond of drinking, and this eventually caught up with him as far as his own reputation was concerned. He also had an illegal encounter with a young girl that found him sentenced to state prison for seven years.[44] Clearly, Hamilton's lack of upstanding character and lack of any connection to the actual incident discredited his narrative.

MR. EDWARD HOPKINS resided in St. Clair County, Michigan, and confessed in 1827 that he knew of all the circumstances surrounding Morgan's death. Hopkins admitted to being present when Morgan was being held in Fort Niagara. He confessed, as well, to setting Morgan adrift in a canoe headed toward the falls. Hopkins admitted that he had tried to save Morgan's life and offered to be responsible for him, but his compatriots would not allow this. Hopkins did not observe who pushed the canoe toward the falls, since he reportedly had turned his back to that act, according to Knight in 1950.[45] Having no corroboration from any other source, the confession was not given any weight.

MR. EDWARD GIDDINS was an important player in the Morgan abduction since he was the first jailer of the powder magazine at Fort Niagara where Morgan was held after his hasty nighttime departure from Canandaigua. The problem with Giddins's story is that it took years for him to provide it and it was also unsupported by external evidence, like those of the aforementioned Hopkins, Hamilton and Hill. It is important to consider that initially, Giddins said nothing regarding Morgan's fate. According to Strong in 1827, Giddins was asked specifically by Lewiston Committee "visitors" in March 1827 if he had seen two individuals involved in moving Morgan to Fort Niagara (Niagara County Sheriff Eli Bruce and William King). Giddins replied that he would answer when he was legally called on to do so. With that, he was apparently told that by not answering, he left the impression that he had seen these individuals; he made no response.

Giddins published a series of anti-Masonic almanacs after 1826, providing piecemeal commentary on the Morgan incident along with other topics of interest. In his 1829 almanac, three years after the incident of Morgan's disappearance, Giddins elaborated on how Morgan had been brought to him late on the night of September 13 (and spilling into the wee hours of

Niagara Falls, New York. *Image license provided by Alamy.com.*

September 14), "hands tied behind him with a cord," for delivery by boat to the Canadian Freemasons who were supposedly prepared to receive him. Giddins admitted that he was the boatman who rowed three others along with Morgan to the Canadian side of the Niagara. He was told to wait offshore with Morgan and one other, while two went to shore and made the final transfer arrangements. After some hours passed, the two returned along with some high-ranking Freemasons of Canada, having determined that Morgan had to be returned to the American side until the Canadians were ready for him. This was when Morgan was locked in the powder house at the fort and thus began his false imprisonment.

According to Giddins, over the next few hours and then days, Morgan became belligerent and noisy, much to Giddins's own chagrin and that of his fellow Freemasons. They attempted to appease Morgan with liquor, assurances and threats, but his mood was volatile and suspicious. Giddins eventually turned over his key to the powder house to another, declaring that he wanted no more to do with the situation. At the end of the day on September 17, Giddins states, he went to York to do some work on the lighthouse there and did not return until September 21. He mentions that upon his return, Morgan was no longer present in the powder house.

Giddins turns to hearsay statements then, saying that at that time, one Freemason told him that Morgan had been murdered, which, to Giddins, indicated that the deed must have occurred on the night of September 19, given that a number of men were seen near Fort Niagara at that time. This Freemason reported that Morgan was absent on the morning of September 20 when he went check on him in the powder house. This same man reported to Giddins that another brother had been seen frequently at the fort during Giddins's absence and had come over in a boat on the evening of September 19, late. This led Giddins to believe that this informant was one of a number who had "sealed the man's doom," as stated in his 1829 publication.[46] This narrative left Giddins with the distinct impression that Morgan had been thrown into the river. Another brother told Giddins on September 22 that Morgan had "undoubtedly been destroyed."[47] Giddins judged both who informed him of these surmises and observations to be in earnest.

Morris, in his 1883 report, adds an important detail regarding Giddins's statement, specifically that he was "paid by the government for his revelation."[48] Today, when a person is paid to offer a particular testimony, they are called a "hired gun." This fact and the delay in the story's being told would raise serious questions about the quality and veracity of the statement for any finder of fact. Recall that investigators value res gestae statements most of all, since those statements have not been worn down by the passage of time, the imagination, calculation and/or coordination with others.

When it came to providing testimony in court—which primarily would have occurred prior to any of his almanacs' publication—Giddins was deemed unreliable in almost all the related trials by all judges that reviewed the case and the accompanying testimony of others. He was considered "not trustworthy and…his unsupported word was valueless," as described by Knight in 1950.[49] The main reason for this is that Giddins professed to be an atheist, which made his statements unreliable in the eyes of any court at the time. Note that to this day, in the twenty-first century, witnesses in the United States take oaths by laying their left hand on a Bible and swearing to tell "the truth, the whole truth, and nothing but the truth." It also implied that, as an atheist, Giddins had lacked candor when he became a Freemason, as belief in a higher power is a requirement.

Giddins did, however, testify in some later trials, after his almanac series was released, where he was allowed as a witness (in 1830, in Niagara County) in order to discuss the custodial arrangements, layout and construction of the powder house where Morgan had purportedly been held. The following year, Giddins testified in the Niagara County trial of Parkhurst Whitney, Timothy Shaw, Noah Beach, William Miller and Samuel M. Chubbuck, who were also accused of conspiring to abduct, imprison and assault/batter William Morgan. Here, his recollection of the details conflicted with information that others had provided regarding how Morgan was treated during his time at Fort Niagara.

Giddins restated the aforementioned incendiary narrative that appeared in his 1829 almanac. For example, Giddins stated that Morgan was "bound" with "hands tied behind him" on the night of September 13, 1826, when Giddins was called on to take him and three other men (Bruce, Hague and King) to the Canadian side of the river (according to the trial transcript of 1831). Yet Sheriff Eli Bruce (Niagara County sheriff and a Freemason) was confident that Morgan was not bound (again according to the trial transcript of 1831). Giddins reiterated that after Morgan became belligerent and disruptive at the fort, he eventually turned his keys over to King. Interestingly, when asked why he had not allowed Morgan to go free before the purported dramatic end, he did not provide an answer.

Giddins's narrative was consistent in that he affirmed that from September 17 through 21, he was "on business" in York, and on his return, he was told by Colonel Jewett (keeper of the keys at that time) that Morgan had been murdered. These were not Jewett's own words, however, and during cross-examination, Giddins had to admit that no one ever told him what happened to Morgan in direct terms and that no one told him Morgan was alive (per the trial transcript from 1831).

Thirty years later, in 1861, Morris made a visit to Giddins, who was living in Lockport, New York. There was consistency in Giddins's narrative when he was asked about what really happened to William Morgan, since Giddins told Morris that

> *he knew nothing of what was finally done to Morgan. When he left him to go to York, Canada, to repair the lighthouse apparatus, Morgan was at the powder-house, but when he returned the man was gone, and he never heard from him afterward.*

This, then, was Giddins's final statement on the issue—a far less dramatic and shocking one but one where there was neither pressure nor money involved. Further, the consistent theme of Giddins's testimony is that he was not present at the time of Morgan's ultimate disappearance. Thus, his only contribution to the story of Morgan's fate was hearsay gathered from others and possibly published for financial gain.

MR. MANN, a blacksmith from Buffalo, charged a Richard Howard with the murder of Morgan. Apparently, Mann had heard from Howard the story of how Morgan was imprisoned in Fort Niagara and Masonic brothers drew lots to determine who would participate in the dispatch of the prisoner. Mann described Howard as distressed about this and said Howard justified his participation as having done his "Masonic duty."[50] Other writings describe Howard as an "English illuminist" who had purportedly been commanded to kill Morgan by the Illuminati. Howard apparently fled the vicinity when the accusation against him was published, which added to the seeming veracity of Mann's story.

However, Mann himself was eccentric and known in the Buffalo area because of his unusual personality. After he made his deposition, he deteriorated mentally and was described as being a "raving maniac" a few months afterward.[51] Thus, without corroboration from outside sources, the public was left with the words of a man who was clearly in mental decline.

MR. HENRY VALANCE purportedly made a deathbed confession to his physician, John L. Emery, MD, that was printed in 1848 by one Elder Stearns. Decades later, in 1869, Reverend Charles Finney, a reputable man who served as president of Oberlin College, published a book on Valance's story, titled *Confession of the Murder of William Morgan by Mr. Henry L. Valance as Taken Down by Dr. John L. Emery of Racine County, Wisconsin in the Summer of 1848* (1869). In this short narrative, Valance tells of his background, stating that he was originally from England and lived in Canada before taking up residence in New York. He became involved in the Morgan situation by way of his membership in the Masonic fraternity, hearing rumors of it first and then coming to understand (again through local talk) that the original plan for Morgan was "silent contempt" and eventually a more active tack: to move him to Canada and on to Europe.[52] However, the captain of the ship that was to take him to Europe suddenly died, and an alternate plan had to be pursued. Valance stated that the powder room keeper of Fort Niagara (possibly Giddins or Jewett, though Valance never mentions his actual name) was receiving threats and complaints from his father-in-law (who was not a Freemason) and thus had to determine a way to get rid of Morgan quickly. This is how the plot to kill him came about. (Note that this is completely inconsistent with Giddins's narrative of turning the key over to William King and leaving the fort to go to York at the height of the crisis.)

A deathbed confession. *Image license provided by Alamy.com.*

Valance relays that he was among eight men who each drew a piece of paper to determine what their role would be in ridding the fort of Morgan. Five papers were understood to be blank, and three had the letter *D* written on them. Each man drew a paper and departed, knowing that if his paper held the letter *D*, he was to return to the fort at midnight. Valance found that his paper was one of those with a *D*, so he returned to the fort at the appointed hour to meet two others, who loaded Morgan into a skiff along with weights that were tied with a strong cord.[53] They rowed to the middle of the Niagara River and fastened the cord just above Morgan's waist. Morgan was told to stand up. Valance stated that the man's back was to him when he pushed him in the middle of the back so that "he fell forward, carrying the weights with him."[54] The men waited for two to three minutes there in the boat and then rowed back to land, shaking hands and departing in their own separate directions.

The same problem came with this narrative, however: it was unsupported by any externally verifiable facts and was at odds with the other confessions of murder or the lesser charges of false imprisonment/kidnapping that have already been referenced, such as those against Giddins. Valance provided no dates, and the timing of the actual crime reported by him is imprecise. Given these discrepancies, his account was discredited by the public. Additional discussion on the murkiness of Valance's confession and the purported deathbed context will follow later in this chapter.

The "confession" of MR. JOHN WHITNEY comes under immediate suspicion when we realize it was put forward not by himself but by none other than Thurlow Weed. Weed relays in his own 1883 autobiography that Whitney confessed to him what had occurred in 1831 and swore him to secrecy. Then twenty-nine years later, at the National Republican Convention in Chicago in 1860, Whitney supposedly asked Weed to come to visit him and write down what he had told him years before. Weed continues that he did not follow up on that request given the excitement about the party nomination process and his disappointment that Abraham Lincoln had been nominated and departed Chicago without having taken the story down.

The story of Whitney's request to speak to Weed in Chicago was a clear misrepresentation of what had transpired, according to Whitney. This exchange was witnessed by Whitney's son-in-law, who vouched for Whitney's recollection that the discussion involved Whitney questioning Weed's accusations and lies, to which Weed only attempted to mollify the clearly frustrated Whitney.

According to Weed's own story, he regretted his oversight and wrote a letter asking a friend and resident of Chicago to interview Whitney in 1861. He bemoans the fact that the letter reached Chicago one week after Whitney's death. It should be noted at this point that Weed was incorrect in so stating, since Whitney did not die in 1861—rather, he died eight years later.

In September 1859, Whitney detailed his story of what occurred to a friend and well-respected Masonic authority, none other than (the oft cited here) Dr. Robert Morris. A summary follows.

Dr. Morris relayed that Whitney "denied emphatically" that he had made any statement to Weed, according to Knight in 1950.[55] Whitney described to Morris how he had been intimately involved in the plan to move Morgan out of Batavia—with the backing of none other than Governor Dewitt Clinton. Whitney personally met with Clinton during August 1826 and thereafter with Morgan on or about September 5, 1826, to offer him money and assistance in exchange for his desistance in the effort to publish information about Masonic rituals, words, grips, etc. Morgan, at that moment, was utterly destitute, admittedly borderline suicidal and being harried by Miller (for the expected pages to be printed?), so he agreed to the plan without hesitation. The "arrest" in Canandaigua, the carriage trip to Fort Niagara, the temporary confinement in the powder magazine was all a consented-to mechanism to remove Morgan (and shortly thereafter, the plan was, his family) from harm's way and to avert the threat he posed to the Masonic brotherhood.

Whitney also detailed confessions that had come from Morgan: e.g., he had never been made a Mason in any lodge, he had contracted with Miller and others to write the exposé on Masonry, he had agreed to destroy the written and printed work as far as possible and he had been treated with kindness by Cheesebro, Whitney and Bruce during his journey to Fort Niagara. In addition, Whitney (apparently a knowledgeable, firsthand witness) elaborated on what occurred with the Canadian brothers in getting Morgan transferred to the other side of the Niagara River. The cooperating parties' thoughts were that they would be able to find him once he was transferred to Canada, since they had planned on sending Lucinda and his two young children to him shortly thereafter.

Whitney admitted to Morris that this was a supreme blunder and, a week after Morgan's disappearance, they realized their giant misstep. Whitney's narrative is the one that makes mention of sending scouts to find Morgan to try to bring him back, due to the growing consternation and misnomers that were facing the local Freemasons at home. According to Whitney, Morgan left the Canadian village where he was first taken within forty-eight hours of arriving there. He sold his horse at Port Hope and vanished into thin air. Whitney supposed it made sense that he had boarded a ship and gone on to another country, but that was the last any of them had ever seen or heard of him, as recorded by Knight in 1950.[56]

MOST OF THESE CONFESSIONS were deemed illegitimate, inaccurate or lacking in some way by those who heard them at the time they were given. Undermining all of them is the lack of any body to demonstrate that a homicide had in fact occurred. Nevertheless, regardless of the fact that there was no corpus dilecti, when it came time to corroborate the details of the confessions, investigators were not able to do so. In some cases, such as that of Valance, the confession came decades after the fact. For the majority of these narratives, we are faced with the question: Why would anyone confess to a crime that he or she did not commit?

Today, we have heard much about coerced false confessions in the context of criminal justice reform—yet none of those confessions listed in this chapter were coerced, either by police or any other person. These were a different type of false confession known as a voluntary false confession, as described by Kassin in 1997 and McCann in 1998, called the "most enigmatic of types of false confessions" by Kassin and Wrightsmen in their 1985 work.[57] A voluntary false confession is a self-incriminating statement offered without external pressure from police, according to Kassin in 1997. Much more research has been done on the coerced type of false confession than the voluntary one; however, we do know something about those who come forward without pressure and bear witness to some act they in fact did not do.

Aebi and Campistol in 2013 discuss voluntary false confessions as emerging from mental health problems or from perceptions of a tangible or intangible benefit.[58] The former was no doubt the case for Mr. Hill, for example, who gave details about the murder he felt so guilty about, yet no one could lend any support for his story. Aebi and Campistol's 2013 study lists a number of anomalous psychological processes that might result in such a confession: e.g., a pathological need for attention, notoriety or self-punishment; a need to expiate guilt over imagined or real acts; or delusions.[59] The authors provide historical examples: two hundred people confessed to kidnapping Charles Augustus Lindbergh Jr. in 1932, and fifty confessed to murdering Elizabeth Short (the Black Dahlia) in 1947, according to Offshe and Leo in 1987. Kassin and Wrightsmen, in 1985, indicate that, in such cases, there may be a "'morbid desire for notoriety' [that] could account for…[the Lindbergh] episode as well as others in which numbers of false confessions are received for widely publicized crimes."[60] Along with Hill, it can be surmised that Mr. Mann was afflicted with some kind of mental impairment, given the notable decline he suffered after his "confession." Kassin and Wrightsmen, also in 1985, indicate that such cases are known among practitioners to occur when individuals are unable to distinguish between fantasy and reality, citing Guttmacher and Weihofen's 1952 work.

The other category that motivates a voluntary false confession, according to Aebi and Campistol's 2013 work, involves a "benefit to the confessor, either tangible or intangible."[61] A tangible benefit might be lessening a potential punishment. An intangible benefit might be the loyalty of a group or the protection of the same, so that a false confession is offered in exchange. The latter is described by these and other authors (such as Beyer in 2000, Krezewinski in 2002 and Sigurdsson and Gudjinson in 1996) in the context of gangs, inmates and juvenile offenders. If we review the behavior of some of the false confessors presented earlier in the chapter, namely Hamilton and Hopkins, we could interpret their actions as seeking an intangible benefit: that is, loyalty to—and thus *from*—the anti-Masonic faction. Giddins, who confessed after years of delay, may also fall into this category—or it is possible that he gained a tangible benefit, if he was in fact paid for his detailed confession.

A deathbed confession, such as the one that came from Valance, is different from the others, since the confessor would seem to have no worldly gain (tangible or intangible) as a goal. Research on deathbed confessions shows that they are readily accepted as necessarily true. Yet this type of confession must be considered in the full context of the confessor's health, since he or she is certainly in an "enfeebled condition" and the "mind of a dying person could seldom be in that clear state so necessary for a strict adhesion to absolute facts."[62] Given this consideration, there has been criticism since the nineteenth century of the credibility of such dying declarations. In *State v. Dickinson* (1877), the supreme court of none other than the state of Wisconsin—where Valance's confession supposedly took place—heard a case on this matter in which the defense stated,

> *This kind of evidence* [is] *not regarded with favor....Several factors could undermine the reliability of dying declarations:*
> 1. *Physical or mental weakness consequent to the approach of death,*
> 2. *Desire for self-vindication, or*
> 3. *Disposition to impute the responsibility for a wrong to another.*

The defense continued that the court must also consider that such a statement is made "in the absence of the accused and [there is] no opportunity for cross-examination," so that such declarations are a "dangerous kind of evidence."[63]

Given these warnings regarding the flaws and potential dangers of deathbed confessions, Valance's statements (transcribed, supposedly, by his medical doctor and then published and republished during the nineteenth century) should not be discounted immediately but assessed as to their quality of detail and corroboration with other known facts. If we treat his deathbed declaration as if it were given by a man of sound mind, can any truth be found in the details?

Today, when voluntary tips are offered to investigators, the totality of circumstances must be considered in order to validate the information provided. This means that the individual giving the tip must be vetted along with the information itself, giving consideration as well to the context and situation in which the information was provided. We know that Valance provided information on his deathbed to a medical doctor, who was his only witness. In order to vet these two individuals, information on their standing in society and any reflection on their characters would be relevant.

Both Henry L. Valance and John L. Emery, MD, are ephemeral personae in official records, such as the U.S. census of the time that they would have been alive in Wisconsin. Relevant state records also are devoid of any listings of these individuals, per today's records and census searches along with communication with the clerk of Racine County, Wisconsin. Of course, it is not at all difficult to imagine that the federal and state censuses may have missed these men during the data collection period, since all censuses and surveys never gather a 100 percent population sampling, and this part of the country was the frontier, with many living in remote and hard-to-access settings. Public census data do show that a "John L. Emery" was born in 1810 in Ohio and died in 1910 in Kansas. Is this our doctor who took the confession from the still more elusive Mr. Valance?

Dr. Emery (possibly the Ohioan documented in public records or whoever he may be) states in his introduction to *Confession of the Murder of William Morgan by Mr. Henry L. Valance* that after deciding to publish the confession, he initially intended to "re-cast" it; however, he realized that if he did so, he would not be complying with the intention of the "author" (Valance), so he had the book printed from the original manuscript as it had been taken down. Thus, we have the words of Valance as transcribed by Emery, said to be unadulterated.

To add further context, the publication of this deathbed account by others—to wit, Elder Stearns and, later, Dr. Charles Finney of Oberlin College, both of whom had clear religious ties to Protestant churches—does suggest that the confession may have been released to the public for the purpose of affecting public opinion.

Intriguingly, a deeper census investigation into the name Henry Valance did result in the discovery of a person born in 1834 in the western New York area. This Mr. Henry Valance is now buried in Mumford Rural Cemetery, having died in 1924. A Vallance Road can still be found in Leroy, New York—the site of the beginning of Morgan's questionable Masonic affiliation.

Further information about Valance's strange confession came to light in a July 25, 1981 story in the *Daily News* of Batavia: one Leatrice J. LaDuke of North Palm Beach, Florida, reported that in sorting through her deceased father's belongings, amid sympathy cards and letters dating back to 1959, she found a black folder. In that folder was a clearly aged envelope with a message in pencil: "This is very old [or odd] and is worth keeping it may be of some value to someone at sometime." The envelope bore the imprint of First National Bank of Batavia and contained a Christmas card and a poorly preserved piece of paper with the header "Confession of Henry L. Valance." The handwriting on the paper is not the same as that on the envelope. LaDuke concluded that this aged document was likely her grandfather's (Mark Johnson of Batavia), passed down to her father (Raymond Arthur Johnson). She was unable to establish any connection between this person, Henry Valance, and her family. She guessed that the paper dated to the 1840s or 1850s, judging by the yellow color of the paper and the handwriting style. Interestingly, the letter had an embossed seal of the United States Congress in its upper left-hand corner. LaDuke added that her father was a Freemason, but she was not sure if her grandfather or great-grandfather (Thomas H. Johnson) were. (It should be mentioned here that the 1981 newspaper story perpetuates the notion that Morgan was a Freemason, was expelled from the brotherhood and then was never seen again, but a body thought to be his was recovered and buried in Old Cemetery on Harvester Road.)

A photocopy of the first page of this "confession" letter of LaDuke's was provided to this author for research purposes by the Town of Pembroke's historian. (The subsequent pages were requested but were not available.) A comparison of the LaDuke letter with the original *Confession of the Murder of William Morgan* of September 11, 1848, published in 1869, reveals differences. To wit, certain punctuation marks and the word "ill-fated" do not appear in the LaDuke letter but do appear in the published version. These differences indicate that the LaDuke letter was not a simple copy of the published Valance confession but was rather some kind of draft version. If this is the case, why does a draft version (stamped by Congress, nonetheless) exist of a "deathbed confession"? Has anyone out there ever heard of someone producing "drafts" of their "deathbed confession"? This LaDuke letter certainly should wake us up to consider the possibility that this "confession" was some kind of coordinated hoax.

Although fraught with uncertainty and without any historical data to confirm the existence of Valance as a Wisconsin resident, if, for argument's sake, the story is accepted as valid for the moment, Valance's narrative should be compared and contrasted to Hopkins's, since he, too, discussed binding Morgan and pushing him into the waters of the Niagara River late at night. Valance provides great detail, although no dates, while Hopkins's description of events differs in many basic elements of what occurred.

Two of the remaining confessors, Giddins and Whitney, were clearly personally involved, as historical documentation and court trial records tell us. Giddins's story was inconsistent, and the timing of his admissions was highly questionable; thus, his value as a potential witness, along with his entire story, has been dismissed by various courts. He no doubt felt guilty about his role as keeper of the powder house—perhaps from early on, when Morgan still lived—and desired to clear his conscience. His admitted absence from the area at the time of Morgan's disappearance assures us that his accounts of Morgan's death are hearsay at best. And the lack of fact corroboration shows us that Giddins was unable to tell his secondhand and indirect story in a convincing way, thus undermining himself.

Whitney, given the extent of detail provided to Morris (1883), seems to be a confessor but not a false confessor. Weed attempted to conjure a false confession, but we see from eyewitness accounts of the Chicago discussion as well as Weed's erroneous information on the death of Whitney (1861 instead of 1869) that it was Weed who provided falsehoods to the public in Whitney's case. Whitney's narrative, with all its in-depth descriptions and corroborated evidence, appears to be the closest to the truth of all the confessors'. Of note, Whitney himself confessed not to murder but to the deportation of Morgan to Fort Niagara.

Chapter 5

THE PEMBROKE SKELETON

What, hath this thing appeared again tonight?
—as spoken by Marcellus in Hamlet, *Act 1, Scene 1*

Time passed, and the Anti-Masonic Party faded and melded into the new Whig Party. Other powerful and divisive forces arose in the nation, leading the citizenry into a bloody civil war, from which it emerged in 1865 profoundly transformed and in need of intense healing.

Reconstruction began without the strong and trusted guiding hand of President Lincoln. Freemasons saw their membership numbers increasing at this time of rebuilding and community-based support, and they contributed to the efforts to support their fellow Americans in the postwar recovery. Lincoln's untimely death undoubtedly set the country on a different and possibly more chaotic course, yet any peace was welcomed, and rebuilding the newly (albeit tenuously) united country was the priority.

Year	Democrats	Republicans	Other
1866	44	147	4
1868	67	171	5
1870	104	139	0
1872	89	203	0
1874	182	103	8
1876	157	136	0
1878	141	132	20
1880	131	151	10

Political party affiliation in the House of Representatives post–Civil War. *Based on Hartman, 2019.*

During this time of national healing, over half a century after Morgan's disappearance, a possible "break" in the case came to light. The *Batavia Daily News*'s top story on June 21, 1881, reported what was touted as a "startling discovery." The story described the discovery of a human skeleton near the town of Pembroke, New York, also in Genesee County, about eleven miles from Batavia. With the skeleton was "evidence that it is none other than the remains of William Morgan, the anti-Masonist who disappeared so mysteriously in 1826."

The details are summarized as follows: A Dr. Phillips (historical records indicate a physician named E.A. Phillips practiced in Pembroke at that time) provided an account, apparently, stating that the find occurred on "Monday of last week," which corresponds to June 13, 1881:

> *While Thos. Egan and Rodney Alexander were engaged in the removal of dirt for the purpose of opening a stone quarry, situated on the farm of Christian Tesno, three miles west of Pembroke, they unearthed the remains of a human body, the bones of which were in an advanced state of decomposition.*

The remains were reportedly found about three rods (one rod is sixteen and a half feet) from the center of the road and about two miles south of the Tonawanda Indian Reservation, "covered with thick layers of dirt and heavy stone." It was thought at first to be a possible "Indian brave"; however, there were no grave goods ("trinkets") to be found, so that possibility was ruled out immediately.

According to the *Daily News*, the workers carefully removed the bones, "placed them to one side" and continued removing dirt by the handful, inspecting it as they continued. This careful filtering revealed a silver ring with the monogram "W.M." as well as a small tin box, similar to a tobacco box. The latter was in dilapidated condition and apparently fell apart when it was removed from its soil matrix. Amazingly, the box "contained writing," which was barely legible. This is where a "Dr. Phillips" comes into the story.

The "manuscript" was taken to Dr. Phillips (and perhaps the ring and remains, though this is not mentioned) who determined that the item "was a piece of paper that had been burned with the remains." Of note, no other mention of burning of the remains has been found. The *Daily News* reported that Phillips took the paper to his house, and while a few words could be read with the naked eye, he used his microscope to see others, such as "Masons," "kill," "liar," "prison" and "Henry Brown." This paper, with such words, was described in the newspaper as "important," since "William Morgan claimed to be in receipt of letters threatening his life unless he stopped his promised exposé." The name "Henry Brown" was seen by the writer as another important link to Morgan, since

> *from the data at hand it seems that a public meeting was called here* [Batavia] *on the 4th of October 1826, for the purpose of making some arrangements in order to ascertain the fate of Morgan. A Mr. Henry Brown took an active part at that meeting. He was an attorney in this place at the time of Morgan's disappearance.*

The reporter summarizes the significance of the manuscript along with other evidence by stating,

> *Now, taking all in, til, this is pretty important testimony and cannot help have some weight. Then there is the ring with the monogram W.M., which taken with the rest makes the evidence stronger. The query now naturally arises from what has been discovered whether this is sufficient evidence to set at rest the long unanswered question, "Where is Morgan?"*

The following day, June 22, 1881, none other than the *New York Times* reported on the astounding find. The *Times* reporter deduced that, given the location provided by the *Batavia Daily News*, the stone quarry referred to was probably that of Mr. W.C. Woolsey. The *Times* was supportive of the *Daily News*'s suggestion that this skeleton was that of William Morgan. To that writer, the case was apparently nearly closed—or as he phrased it, "the mystery…seems to be unraveled at last."

Along with the description of the disposition of the remains and the monogrammed ring and dilapidated tin box, the *New York Times* story elaborates on the aged pages that were reviewed by Dr. Phillips and the words he was able to discern upon magnification. The name Henry Brown is mentioned and detailed further by the *Times*, stating that Brown was "a lawyer in this town and a prominent Mason." Brown's 1829 book, cited here in chapter 3, is mentioned as a work that admits that Morgan was abducted, most likely by Masons, but was not murdered by them or anyone else; the article continues that in that book, Brown "indulges" himself to go on and say that the entire episode was uncalled-for, "the work of political demagogues." According to the *Times*, Brown should now be considered one of Morgan's murderers, given the finds in the quarry. Brown had long ago died in Chicago, in 1849, and had no way to defend his name or his honor. The *Times* continued that "this discovery bids fair to explode all other theories regarding to the fate of Morgan."

A detailed recap of the Morgan affair follows—as a reminder or an alert to those who were not alive or around at the time. The "light sentences" given to the four who were charged and tried are also discussed. The discovery of what were thought to be Morgan's remains in Lake Ontario is revisited, with the caveat that Sarah Munro's identification of the clothing indicated that decomposing body was that of Timothy Munro and not Morgan. Surprisingly, the reporter states that "very many of the citizens of Batavia" still believe that the remains were those of Morgan and that a "movement was started last month" to raise a monument to William Morgan "in the cemetery in which those bones are buried." Clearly the reporter was not aware that Munro's remains had been taken to Canada after the third inquest in 1827.

THE PRINTING PRESSES WERE apparently reignited at this time to affect public opinion, relying on poorly preserved personal effects reportedly found with skeletal remains. The biological evidence was completely ignored by Dr. Phillips, the only apparent medical/scientific authority involved in this case.

Today, when all that remains of a body are skeletal remains, a forensic anthropologist is called in to assist. Clearly, the standards of forensic anthropological assessment of remains are much higher today than they were in the late nineteenth century; however, there were basic analyses that could have been performed in order to attempt to confirm or deny, scientifically, the biological profile of those remains.

For example, as the 1827 inquests demonstrated, the biological profile of the remains can be compared/contrasted with what is known of the missing person. The stature of a person can be calculated by measurement of the skeletal remains; this was not done with any regularity until the mid-twentieth century, using the Fully (1956) method, for example. Yet other anthropometric methods (known as Bertillonage or the Bertillon system, after Alphonse Bertillon) were coming into regular use and standardization in Europe and the United States at this time. The Bertillon system of body measurements was employed for living individuals in order to individualize them from others for law enforcement and criminal investigation purposes. It was known that bone measurements could provide similar yet more general information about a skeleton in order to rule individuals in or out.

For skeletal remains devoid of flesh, measurements of particular bones were being developed and refined but had not yet been published (see Rollet, 1889, and Manouvrier, 1892).

Determinations of sex and, possibly, ancestry/bio-affinity could be and were in some cases made at that time using the skull. The adult male skull demonstrates relatively more rugose muscle attachment sites on the brow, mandible (lower jaw bone), mastoid processes (bony protuberances behind the ear) and occipital bone (posterior bone of the skull). For bio-affinity, various bony features of the mid-face, such as the eye sockets, nasal opening and maxilla (upper jaw), were considered to be indicative of environmentally shaped adaptations of our ancestors.

The second and third inquests revealed that Morgan had undergone surgical debridement of a frostbitten toe. As mentioned in chapter 2, such surgically induced trauma on bone could be detected by observers, especially with the aid of a medical microscope (as Dr. Phillips had). Such cut marks, if found, would lend themselves to the building of a circumstantial identification of William Morgan.

One can also note when reading the news reports about this find that the lack of "trinkets" was used as an indicator that this skeleton is not that of a Native American. In more technical language, this means that

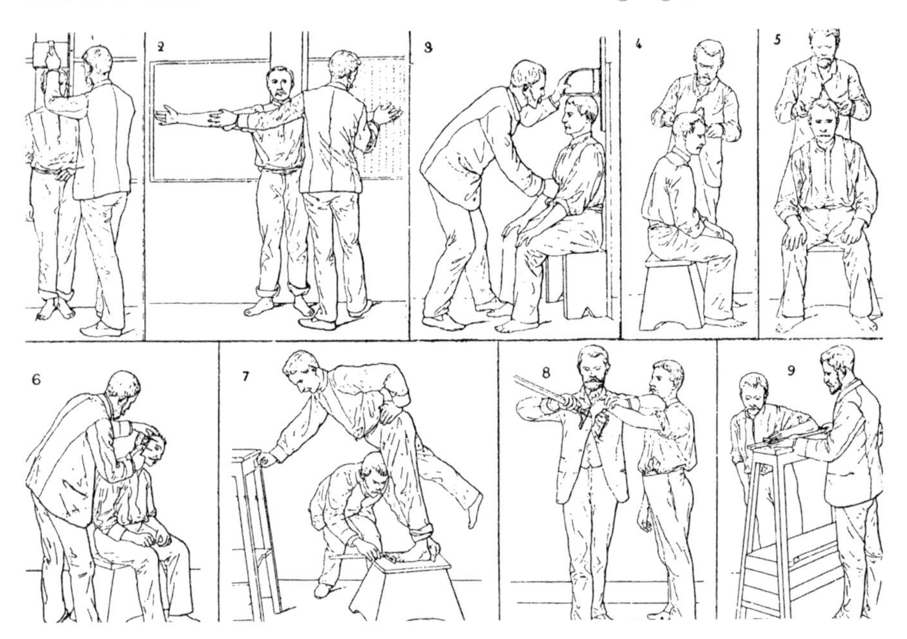

The Bertillon anthropometric method. *Image license provided by Alamy.com.*

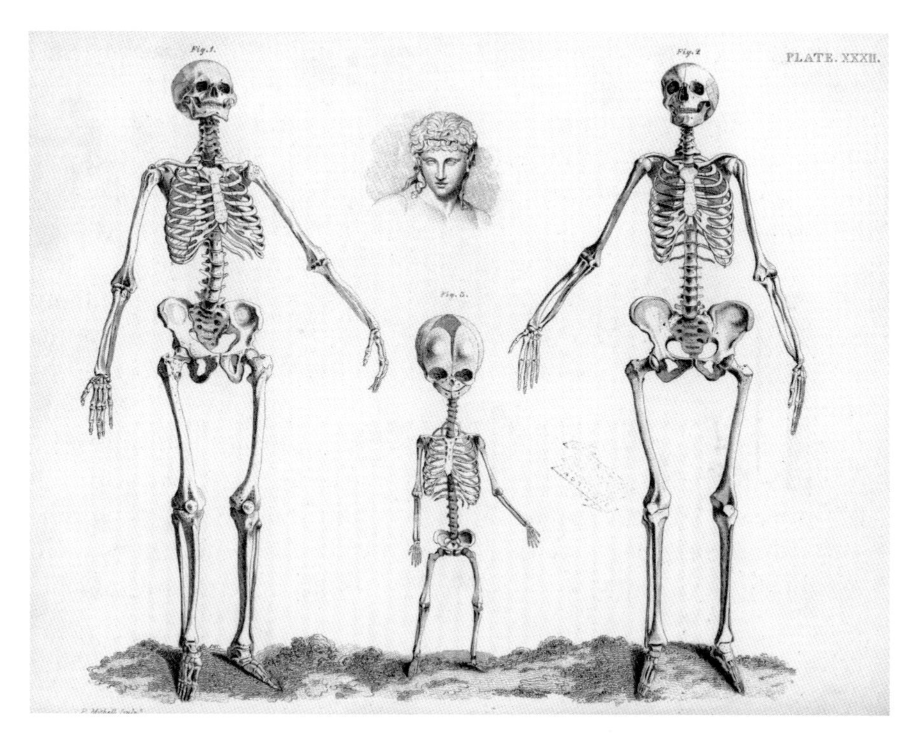

Nineteenth-century male versus female versus child skeletal comparative diagram. *Image license provided by Alamy.com.*

no Native American artifacts—such as ritual-related grave goods like jewelry, smoking paraphernalia, weapons and the like—were recovered. As the old investigative mantra goes, "Absence of evidence is not evidence of absence." Thus, the mere fact that this particular burial was devoid of Native artifacts does not necessarily mean that the remains were not those of an Indigenous person. However, consideration of contextual clues is important and still done today when skeletal remains are found in unattended death cases. The presence of grave goods is clearly a helpful clue that the remains discovered probably date to prehistoric times. Likewise, the inclusion of early pioneer artifacts such as coffin nails cannot be ignored as a temporal indicator of a historic burial.

Even if the skeletal features of the individual were not analyzed using the science of the day, the unique dental features known about William Morgan could have been employed immediately in order to rule the skeleton in as being "possibly William Morgan." As discussed in chapter 2, double teeth are uncommon and noticeable even to the layperson. Yet Dr. Phillips, observers at the time and thus the media made no mention of dental markers, simply focusing on the historical artifacts found and what these implied.

The keys to this purported identification are the engraved ring and the dilapidated box with the burned "manuscript." For now, let us state that today, personal effects are not used for positive identification of skeletal remains, yet they may be used for circumstantial identification. The difference between these two is that the former, positive identification, uses methods that each stand alone and require no supporting evidence to confirm identity (e.g., dental and nuclear DNA). The latter, circumstantial identification, employs multiple forms of evidence, none of which alone is strong enough to support the identification (stature, sex, age at death, personal effects) yet all of which, considered together, make a case for an identification.

Yet personal effects in the past—even up to and including the time of World War II—were relied on to establish identity without corroboration. For example, a soldier's remains could be identified on the battlefield with the use of dog tags alone. This was eventually regarded as flawed, since dog tags could be traded, mixed up or disassociated with remains (in case of an explosion or a multi-person vehicle accident or burial in a mass grave, for example). So criticism of the use of these personal effects found in the Pembroke quarry grave for identification purposes is moot, given the standards of the day. Again, remember that the lack of artifacts was seen as proof that the skeletal remains were not those of a Native American ("Indian brave"). It was as if the bones and teeth were completely uninformative to the observer—but this was not the case, even in those early days of identification science. Recall that the narrative states that the biological remains were "set aside" as digging continued.

Not only the excavation's context but also the larger social and political climate should be considered here in the Pembroke quarry case, as was done at the time of Morgan's disappearance. Why the sudden media report in a local and then a large, reputable national newspaper? Was there any reason for this beyond the desire to close a case that had been unsolved? Why would normal procedure not be followed, as in the coroners' inquests described in chapter 2? As aforementioned, Morgan had double teeth, which could and should have been employed even in a skeletonized case for identification purposes. As mentioned previously, the debridement of his toe may have left cut marks that could and should have been used (if present) to build a circumstantial identification. These relatively rare features were not described in the news story.

All media were not on the same page, however. Some local newspapers approached the discovery differently. For example, the weekly *Medina Tribune*, on June 24, 1881, published no report in its pages on the subject, yet the village of Medina is located only sixteen miles from the quarry where the bones and artifacts were found. Instead, a "Masonic Lesson" was printed:

You were taught while an Apprentice
To stand upright and be square,
Ever watchful of your actions
Always just and always fair;
Ever mindful that a craftsman
Should be seeking but to learn;
That the honors of the future
You should well and truly learn.

When you passed the Middle Chamber,
And a Craftsman were become,
Did you heed the lesson taught you,
Take the lisp from out your tongue,
So that when you've passed o'er Jordan
And unto the Lodge above,
You can give the Password promptly,
And secure the Master's love?

When, my brother, you ascended
From the Level to the Square,
And became a Master Mason,
Did you learn a lesson there?
Did the Truth in all its beauty,
Touch the chord within your heart,
Making you like Master Hiram,
There resolve to do your part,
So that when the Great Grand Master
Should you summon from afar,
Your Trestle Board will indicate
And all your work is at par?

—Times-Star, *Cincinnati*

These words are immediately followed by a poem by prohibition advocate Mary Lathrap titled "Dead March":

Tramp, tramp, tramp, in the drunkard's way,
March the fact of a million men;
If none shall pity and none shall save,
Where will the march they are making end?
The young, the strong, and the old are there,
In woeful ranks as they hurry past,
With not a moment to think or care,
What is the fate that comes at last?

Tramp, tramp, tramp, to a drunkard's doom,
Out of boyhood pure and fair,
Over the thoughts of love and home,
Past the check of mother's prayer,
Onward swift to a drunkard's crime,
Over the plea of wife and child,
Over the holiest ties of time,
Reasons dethroned, and soul gone wild.

Tramp, tramp, tramp, will a drunkard's grave.
Covers the broken life of shame,
While the spirit of Jesus died to save,
Meets a future we dare not name;
God helps us all—there's a cross to bear
And work to do for the mighty throng;
God give us strength till the toil and prayer
Shall end one day in the victor's song.

Might the story's omission, along with the presentation of these creative works, have a connection to the resurrection of the Morgan story over half a century later? The editor and sole proprietor of the *Medina Tribune* at the time was Frank H. Hurd, an upstanding citizen, according to all historical reports, and a "prominent Mason, belonging to the Chapter at Albion and the Genesee Commandery at Lockport, NY."[64] Was the public seeing, or not seeing, stories based on the editors' views on the matter?

Freemasons had their own publication, which addressed the matter directly, however. The *Freemasons Chronicle* (June 25, 1881) discussed the story as reported by another publication, the *Standard*, in a short commentary piece titled "The Morgan Mystery." The circumstances of the discovery are reviewed and the *Standard* article directly quoted in parts. In the end, the author makes a suggestion about why the Morgan mystery is being rehashed:

> *It is only natural that this alleged discovery of Morgan's skeleton has been the cause of the most intense excitement throughout the whole State of New York. At the same time a most curious coincidence must not be entirely overlooked. The* Standard *correspondent writes that "there has been, this year, a movement to erect a monument in Batavia to Morgan," and in the circumstances, nothing better could have happened than the discovery of his skeleton. The skeleton—always, be it understood, in the supposition that it is the veritable skeleton of William Morgan—cannot fail to prove an excellent basis on which to erect a monument to perpetuate his fame or infamy.*

A modern historian, Keene, in 2011, follows up on this seemingly explosive news story, stating that ultimately the bones were never linked with Morgan. To date, no official report has been discovered by this author—requests to the county clerk revealed this absence. Of course, at the time, there was no DNA testing available. As has been mentioned in this chapter, Keene also discusses the use of dental comparisons during two of the inquests in 1827 (as detailed here in chapter 2). Why were these not used with the quarry skeleton? The grave inclusions are also not discussed further by Keene, yet those were the strongest "evidence" cited at the time as a link to Morgan. What became of the engraved ring and the metal box with incendiary text? These being offered as the missing links to solve the mystery of Morgan, should they not be ensconced in a museum for all to see? Why, if they are of such great import, were they not committed to historical preservation? Or is it that, ultimately, they were discovered to be less than crucial after all? The lack of any report, remains or artifacts from the quarry tells us much. A Google Maps search of the vicinity of this incident today reveals a quarry or notable depression feature at 43 degrees 01' 43" N, 78 degrees 27' 04" W, at an elevation of 250.49 meters, situated approximately 200 meters north of Tesno Road. Would this not be a place to demarcate with a historical sign or marker if such a ground-breaking discovery had been made? Needless to say, no such marker exists.

It would be remiss not to mention a historical moment of national upheaval that occurred very near in time to the Pembroke quarry discovery: the assassination of President James A. Garfield on July 2, 1881. Historians tell us that President Garfield, who was just four months into his first term, was shot at the Baltimore and Potomac Railroad Station on that day at 9:30 a.m. He survived the injury for seventy-nine days, dying on September 19, 1881. The assassin was identified as Charles J. Guiteau, who could be termed "disgruntled" by his own admission but is often described as "mentally ill." Guiteau's own book, titled *The Truth and The Removal*, explains how he was inspired by Almighty God to commit this violent act.

President James A. Garfield. *Image license provided by Alamy.com.*

In the context of the Morgan mystery, it is intriguing that James Garfield was one of the few U.S. presidents in the late nineteenth century who was in fact a Freemason. He became a Master Mason in Columbus Lodge 30 in Columbus, Ohio, in 1864. As a member of Congress and residing in Washington, D.C., for part of the year, Garfield was affiliated with Pentalpha Lodge No. 23 as one of its charter members in 1869.

Is this a random coincidence or an indication of hidden political forces at work to set up a national narrative regarding the dubiousness of Masonic leadership? The quarry skeleton's discovery prior to the presidential assassination suggests coincidence, yet anti-Masonic forces still very much at work in American circles of power could seize on this as fuel for their favorable fire. Recall the Machiavellian tenet used by Thurlow Weed in the time of Morgan: never let a crisis go to waste.

A cursory investigation into Guiteau's background shows that he was politically affiliated with Ulysses S. Grant's unsuccessful reelection campaign in 1880. When Garfield emerged as the Republican nominee, Guiteau threw his support behind him, hoping for political favor. The lack of any political appointment or payback led to his anger, according to the historical narrative. In addition, an ongoing and divisive effort to reform the civil service of the federal government had produced a highly toxic political atmosphere at the time, so that a disturbed individual saw himself as the person chosen (by the "Deity") to put an end to this factional and personal dispute. His own aforementioned written confession indicates an apparent motivation by otherworldly forces. Since an empirical, investigative approach is taken here, we must rely on Guiteau's own writings as well as historical reports: that is, Guiteau was a disturbed individual with a real or imagined grudge held against Garfield.

As we have already seen in chapters 1 and 3, the honorary monument was erected one year after the Pembroke skeleton came to light. The imposing figure of William Morgan was raised to its heights on September 13, 1882, (notably, the same day that Morgan disappeared in 1826) in a ceremony witnessed by an estimated one thousand onlookers, including local Masonic lodge members. The monument was sponsored by the National Christian Association (NCA) of Chicago with national and international funding; undoubtedly, some of the monies were generated from the emotions stirred by the skeleton find. What more do we know about the National Christian Association of Chicago, which organized for and paid $20,000 derived from fundraising efforts and contributions toward the monument?

The NCA was a group based primarily on opposition to secret societies. According to the historical records of Wheaton College, the NCA arose in reaction to the survival of Masonic lodges into the mid-nineteenth century. The NCA emerged in the 1860s, with the inspiration and encouragement of Free Methodist ministers N.D. Fanning and C.H. Underwood. These leaders developed tracts, lectures and sermons to expose the deep concerns they held about secret societies and the conflict that they saw between secret societies and the freedom of Jesus Christ in his open ministry that he performed. The NCA established a publishing arm in 1868, the *Christian Cynosure*, warning even more Christians about "secretism," including the Elks, the Oddfellows, and eventually Mormonism, Christian Scientism, even Communism. The NCA, in its efforts to quash secret societies, revived the Anti-Masonic Party in 1872.

The driving force of this publication was Jonathan Blanchard, the first president of Wheaton College. He considered Freemasonry a diabolical institution second only to slavery. The previously cited Charles Finney (president of Oberlin College and publisher of the Valance confession first published by Emery) became another strong proponent of the NCA and the *Christian Cynosure*, since he was a third degree Freemason who reportedly soured on Freemasonry and "converted to Christ."[65] Another prominent figure in the 1860s was Edmond Ronayne, who would expose and deride Masonic rituals and teachings in public presentations around the country. Ronayne, too, was a former Freemason who turned away from his oath and followed a different path that he envisioned as proper.

The NCA's push against secret societies focused especially on Freemasons in the latter half of the nineteenth century. Erecting a public monument at the heart of the place where, and on the calendar date when, the unsolved mystery began served as a reminder and reinforced in the collective consciousness the suspicious nature of such groups. Could there be any other purpose, other than saving souls and encouraging open reverence to God, for this revival of the dark and gloomy Morgan affair?

The short answer to that question is yes. The main energy behind the NCA, Jonathan Blanchard, put forward his name for none other than president of the United States for the 1884 election, two years after the Batavia cemetery ceremony. His party affiliation was originally Anti-Masonic; however, he unsuccessfully ran for president as a candidate of the American Prohibition Party, which was the successor of the new Anti-Masonic Party. It seems the spirit of Thurlow Weed had awakened, to stir the voting public with a skeletal, and then graven, "good enough Morgan" before an election yet again.

Thus the Pembroke skeleton emerged as William Morgan for a moment in time—identified, albeit circumstantially, by the personal effects found with it in its quarry grave. The missing persons case of the century was supposedly solved, yet no remains, ring or documents exist as evidence today. These, oddly, faded into the past, almost as quickly as they came to public attention. They remain thus nothing but rumor or hearsay.

Yet rumor begets rumor. In a February 16, 2008 news report, journalist Scott DeSmit of the Batavia *Daily News* uses the Pembroke bones to conclude: "Genesee oldest, coldest case solved at last." He determines by his own review of the journalist's report of the Pembroke quarry skeleton that Morgan was "in Pembroke all along." DeSmit states that he wishes he could take credit for solving this "181-year-old mystery but the credit goes to editor Ray Coniglio, who found an article from the *New York Times* dated June 22, 1881." DeSmit contributes to the ongoing Morgan rumors by writing in his summary background of the case, "In 1826, Morgan wrote Morgan's *Illustrations of Masonry*, a book betraying the secrets of the Masons and one that likely got him killed."

Chapter 6

WHAT BECAME OF WILLIAM MORGAN?

Since William Morgan's remains have never been recovered, his case is still technically a cold missing persons case. As discussed in chapter 1, modern-day investigators know that a variety of circumstances can result in a missing person, so there is no mandatory waiting period to file a missing persons report. However, many agencies will not consider starting an investigation until an adult has been gone for a certain period, since approximately 70 percent of all reported missing persons are found or voluntarily return within forty-eight to seventy-two hours—undoubtedly, many of these intentional runaways. Some circumstances surrounding Morgan's disappearance suggest that Morgan may have been someone who willingly vanished from his deteriorating home life in 1826, especially if we weigh the extremely detailed narrative of Whitney against the spotty, vague and uncorroborated stories of others.

Investigators today would certainly ask: Did William Morgan desire to be taken away by the Freemasons who offered him a reprieve from the growing local tension? When Whitney met with him that fateful night in September to make him the proposal of resettlement in Canada, Morgan was reportedly disheveled in appearance, admitting he had been in an altercation with Miller. Further, Morgan at that time confided in Whitney that he had considered suicide. A change would seem welcome to a man in such a predicament.

Recall that Whitney indicated that Morgan was distraught during their September 1826 meeting, given that pressures were building from not only the local Freemasons for him to cease and desist from the threatened publication but also from Miller and compatriots, urging him to deliver the "goods" for quick printing and publication. The reasons to be extricated from this situation, given the chance, seem plentiful.

Keeping in mind that Morgan could have been a party to the planning and execution of his own "disappearance," other rumors and hypotheses emerged about what became of him. Some are discussed in chapter 1 to demonstrate the wild speculation that ran rampant in western New York communities following his mysterious exit. In this chapter, these narratives will be explored in more detail in order to determine if any seem to have viability and validity.

Voorhis, in 1946, attempts to list exhaustively the rumors—or hearsay reports, in legal language—regarding Morgan's fate. They are summarized below with added commentary in parenthesis:

1. Morgan departed via the St. Lawrence River by boat from Port Hope, Canada. (This was mentioned by Whitney to Morris.) This information came from the two scouts.
2. Morgan became a hermit in northern Canada. (This suggestion does not conflict drastically with Whitney's statements, since Whitney surmised only that Morgan boarded a ship.)
3. Morgan changed his surname to Wanamaker and settled in the vicinity of Albany, New York.
4. Morgan ended up in Boston, Massachusetts, and lived the rest of his life there. (This narrative does not conflict with Whitney's description of events.)
5. Morgan was hanged as a pirate in 1838 in Havana. (This does not conflict with Whitney's description of events.)
6. Morgan became an Indian chief in Arizona.
7. Morgan was sighted in Smyrna (now Izmir), Turkey, between 1828 and 1831 by American sailors. He was wearing Turkish clothing and went by the name of Mustapha. (Again, this narrative does not conflict with Whitney's description of events.)
8. Morgan's boots were discovered in the guts of a lake sturgeon that had washed up on Lake Ontario's shores, indicating that he had been murdered and/or drowned. (This does not conflict with the stories of Valance, Giddins, Hopkins and Mann.)
9. Morgan was thrown overboard, hands tied, in the Niagara River by a group of Freemasons. (This was Valance's story, as well as Giddins's and Mann's.)

10. Morgan was placed in the hollow beneath a partially uprooted tree, and the tree was lowered back in position to cover his remains.
11. Morgan was set adrift in a canoe and sent over Niagara Falls. (Hopkins's story.)
12. Morgan was killed by a man (R.H. Hill), who confessed to the murder and was later ruled to be insane.
13. Morgan was shipwrecked near Cuba, went to the Cayman Islands and lived in the vicinity for the rest of his days.[66] (This narrative does not conflict with Whitney's description of events.)

Morris, in 1883, adds a few additional hypotheses to Voorhis's 1946 list, to wit:

14. A sea captain living in Bridgewater, Massachusetts, reported that he had taken Morgan as a passenger to Antwerp, Holland, in the fall of 1826. He had seen him afterward, "once or twice." Morgan was apparently involved in the business of marketing Holland gin.[67] (This does not conflict with Whitney's story.)
15. In 1840, near Russellville, Kentucky, a man died who was known among the local people to be William Morgan. He had lived there in seclusion, with great concern for his life.[68]
16. A Captain William Morgan was said to be the master of a "trading coaster" in England that ran from Liverpool to Southhaven. This ship was, after ten to fifteen years, lost at sea.[69] (This does not conflict with Whitney's description of events.)
17. Morgan was jailed by Weed and kept, if needed, as a last-resort witness while the local drama played out in western New York. When it was sensed that his presence would do more harm than good, he was murdered with a heavy dose of laudanum added to his rum.[70]

Other rumored "sightings" of Morgan show him emerging in Spain as an officer of Don Carlos, in Long Island as a market gardener and in Mexico City, as reported by none other than General Santa Anna himself.[71]

According to Voorhis, the only one of these narratives accompanied by any supporting evidence is no. 13. Here, we will address each one and detail what was done to vet the information (if any) that was provided at the time. Morris, it should be added, views all with scrutiny; however, notably, he makes no mention of no. 13; Voorhis's Cayman Islands "lead," which must have arisen after Morris's 1883 publication. In addition to concurrent vetting that may have been conducted by investigators then, the availability of digital archival records, such as census data, genealogical information, marriage and immigration records, etc. allows modern-day researchers to vet more widely past allegations. Whenever possible, such online sources were employed in order to check claims made about Morgan's fate.

The first story of what happened to Morgan implies that he arrived on the other side of the Niagara River in Upper Canada and made his way to Port Hope to locations unknown after embarking on a boat on the St. Lawrence River. This narrative does not really tell us what ultimately happened to Morgan; rather, it simply indicates that he was not murdered and lived beyond the Niagara River trip. The only support for this hearsay is oral communications that were later written down. Key among these is the detailed account of John Whitney (according to Morris in 1883), who was admittedly deeply involved in the entire matter, leading up to and including Morgan's false imprisonment at Fort Niagara, the two scouts' search for Morgan once he was liberated on the Canadian side of the river and the reports that they gave on their return. Whitney's detailed and intimate knowledge of the affair, with actual calendar dates provided, lends relative credence to his narrative. As noted, many of the other suggestions about what became of Morgan are not mutually exclusive of this narrative.

Rumors abounded that Morgan had made it across the river and been paid some money by his prior captors, offered a horse by the Canadian "conspirators" and headed off toward the east after less than forty-eight hours. It should be noted that this was a breach of the agreement he had supposedly made with Whitney et al. He was expected to remain in Hamilton for some days. Of course, most of those involved likely thought he would remain in place to receive his wife and children, who were said to be forthcoming.

Morgan Becomes a Hermit

A few of the narratives put forward by Morris and Voorhis can be lumped into this category. The second proposition, that Morgan became a hermit in Canada, has no accompanying evidence to support it. No publicly available archival evidence of Morgan's presence in Canada after his disappearance in September 1826 has been found or reported. Morris adds to this story, stating that the appearance of the man—his bald head and general characteristics—was "identical" to Morgan's.[72] He goes on to say that this recluse whispered his true identity—as *the* William Morgan—into the ear of a sympathizing friend during his last moments.[73] Here is another deathbed confession of sorts, unable to be cross-examined or verified in any way.

An alternative Morgan-as-hermit report has Morgan taking the pseudonym Wanamaker and ending up living in a "low-down shanty" near Albany, according to Morris in 1883.[74] Apparently, logistical support from some of his associates (namely Thurlow Weed and then Governor Seward) drew attention to this locale. The rumor continues that this "gin-soaked creature" threatened to reveal the secret of his true identity, and Weed and Seward strangled him and disposed of his body in a deep, unused well.

In order to determine if there was any record of such a person's presence in that vicinity, examination of the 1830 U.S. census reveals five heads of household in this area of New York State with the name Wanamaker (using this exact spelling). All these listed heads of household (Henry, Harmon, Jacob, Henry and Adolphus) provided records of other members of the household, ranging from three to eleven in number. Thus, none of these represent a single male living on his own and are unlikely to be a "new and improved" version of William Morgan. If alternate spellings of Wanamaker are reviewed (e.g., Wanemaker), the same pattern results, with five heads of household listed in the Albany vicinity (John, Abraham, James, Peter, Lawrence), all noting associated family members ranging from two to eleven in number. No solitary Wanamaker or Wanemaker is listed in the 1830 U.S. census.

The final Morgan-living-the-life-of-a-hermit story is based in the countryside of Kentucky (no. 15) and offers a similar narrative as the Canadian story. This, too, however, is seemingly a baseless rumor with no known hard evidence supporting it. A check of online census data does not support it. A William Morgan is listed in the 1850 and 1870 censuses near Russellville, first in District No. 2, Logan County. Yet this Morgan is a head of household with a wife and four children. In 1870, it appears this same William Morgan lived in Adairsville, working as a farmer, with the same family members listed.

Morgan Returns to Life at Sea

Other narratives can be grouped under this heading. Since Morgan was rumored to have been a seaman and possibly a pirate from the southern waters of the country, these offerings have him returning to his swashbuckling roots, as it were.

A "Morgan as pirate" (no. 5) account stems from a hearsay report of a Guiliem Ganmore (perhaps an attempted anagram for William Morgan) who was a (real or imagined?) pirate in the Caribbean. He was hanged in Havana in 1838, but before that final act, he told the prison priest that he was *the* William Morgan. Again, keep in mind the discussion from chapter 4 of deathbed confessions: their inability to be cross-examined makes them suspect. It should be noted that there is also a verified pirate by the name of Henry Morgan who lived two centuries before the rumored and unverified pirate William Morgan. No records were found that confirmed or denied the Morgan-as-pirate "lead."

Morgan as captain of a "trading coaster" (no. 16) between the English cities of Liverpool and South Haven is another of the wild return-to-sea suggestions without any backing in reality yet likely emerging from the old rumors of Morgan's dashing military adventure in New Orleans, as liberated pirate turned captain. A William Morgan is listed in the 1841 United Kingdom census who lived in Liverpool, a head of household with a wife named Catherine. He was aged sixty-five, which makes him approximately the same age as our William Morgan, as well. This Morgan lists himself as "shoe m," however, not ship captain, and this William Morgan was not an immigrant but a native British citizen.

Morgan Reinvents Himself

A number of narratives hold that Morgan ran away from his temporary Canadian drop-off point and settled down as a trader or entrepreneur, while reinventing his identity with costume, pseudonym or both.

The first report (no. 4) has Morgan ending up in Boston, Massachusetts, and living his life out there. This could be related to, and is not mutually exclusive of, Whitney's testimony that Morgan boarded a steamer from Port Hope and sailed off, in this case to Boston. However, there has been no documentary evidence of his presence in Boston, albeit there are rumors of correspondence between him and Lucinda, the former being in Boston at the time (1827), as well as hints that Morgan continued to contact his fellow publication conspirators there (i.e., Dyer, Davids and Miller). These three apparently made frequent trips to Boston, according to Knight.[75] In addition, an eyewitness named Mr. Brown, a gentleman from Batavia, while on business in Boston observed a person he thought to be Morgan—partially in disguise, however—on the streets. (Is this the same Mr. Henry Brown who is referenced in chapter 5 as the person whose name appears on the burnt "manuscript" from the Pembroke quarry and was framed as Morgan's possible killer?) As told by Stone, apparently Brown called him by name, and the man

> *appeared somewhat disconcerted at first; but drew his cloak close around his face, and turned off into another street. He was pursued for some distance, through various streets and alleys, and ultimately avoided a positive disclosure, by losing himself in a crowd of people.*[76]

Two newspapers published this story, one in Boston and one in Pawtucket, indicating support for the belief that Morgan was in Boston, living incognito and working on a book deal for publication in Spanish.

Another report (no. 6) has Morgan somehow progressing westward to settle; this was based on only the rumor of an incident in 1876, in which an Indian chief named San Procope confessed on his deathbed that he was in fact William Morgan, as told by Morris in 1883.[77] There seems to be a pattern here.

A third, this time quite detailed, Morgan "2.0" report (no. 7), which has him being sighted in Smyrna, Turkey, between 1828 and 1831 by reputable American sailors, comes from statements of those eyewitnesses to support this "lead." The aforementioned statement by a Mr. Brown, who claimed to have seen Morgan on the streets of Boston, soon appeared in a Boston publication, supposedly leading Morgan to become alarmed. He decided to set out for a foreign country in which he could continue to live incognito. He is said to have found a ship (named *America*) headed to Asia Minor, specifically Smyrna (now Izmir), Turkey, and departed under the command of a Captain Waterman. Two signed statements have emerged by the two sailors, Masters and Hitchcock, who stated in 1875 that they did see Morgan in Turkey in 1830. Both men were said to be honest and honorable men with no reason to produce false claims, neither being a Freemason. They both claimed in separate statements that they had encountered an English-speaking man (American) while in Smyrna during their military service. Masters, who reportedly saw Morgan in 1830, noted that the mysterious man had physical qualities matching those of Morgan (including the double teeth "in front") and reported his observation to the United States consul at Smyrna. The consul confirmed that this man had come from Boston about the time Morgan went missing.

Hitchcock's statement aligns well with Masters's: the former also said that he saw Morgan in 1830, wearing Turkish garb and seeming content in his new homeland. Hitchcock reported in his statement that he never saw this man a second time, but others on his ship frequently did see him.

Morris, in 1883, reports that at the time of his book's publication, these two "ancient" seamen were still alive, living in Salem, Massachusetts. He adds that they had indicated in their report that Morgan was involved in commerce there as a "wholesale fruit dealer, largely interested in figs."[78] Morris dismisses this report out of hand, calling it a "figment" and "rumor."

No additional sightings were reported after 1830. Online searches for grave locations of any person using that name in the area of Smyrna yield no results. Of course, if William Morgan used a pseudonym as he was said to have done (Mustapha), then tracking him would be impossible. After the fall of the Ottoman Empire, all surviving records from Smyrna would have been transferred to Istanbul. To date, no records of Morgan's existence in Turkey have been discovered online in a searchable form. Could it be that the two seamen had a "desire for notoriety," as the false confessors may have, as discussed in chapter 4? The delay in reporting this seemingly major incident is also a factor which weakens their statements, from an investigator's standpoint.

Another reinvented Morgan is touched on in Morris's (1883) additional suggestions (all of which he discredits out of hand as mere scuttlebutt, and all of which do not gain support from documentation or evidence today). This one (no. 14) has Morgan turning up in Antwerp, Belgium. It is difficult to trace where this idea came from except that Morgan was involved in commerce with liquor (gin) and this was something he had done before in Canada (run a tavern) as well as a substance for which he was well known to have a fondness (liquor). However, an online search for any listing of William Morgan in any available records from that area did not end in a positive result.

Voorhis's (no. 13) discussion of the reinvented Morgan in the Caribbean Sea combines the Morgan-returns-to-sea and Morgan-reinvents-himself themes and will be presented separately below.

Morgan Is Murdered

Numerous reports indicated that William Morgan met his end soon after his false imprisonment at Fort Niagara. Notwithstanding the lack of a body to this day, we will consider each here, based on its merits under the "totality of circumstances" standard.

The story (no. 8) involving boots found inside a lake sturgeon appeared to be no more than a "fish tale," according to Knight's 1950 work. Sturgeon in the Great Lakes are long-lived, large fish, over seven feet long in some cases, yet their usual fare is live, soft food such as insect larvae, worms, leeches and other small organisms that live in the muddy lake bottoms. The mouth of such a fish is more like a vacuum, in that it is devoid of teeth. It is not impossible but hard to imagine a sturgeon ingesting a human body or large portions of one, such as lower limbs.

Likewise, the partially uprooted tree explanation has had no concrete support arise or corroboration from any other source or party.

Being thrown overboard in the Niagara River (no. 9) was the main explanation for Morgan's disappearance that was promoted and, at least publicly, believed by those who clamored for the Masons to be held accountable for his "murder"—although no charges were ever filed against anyone for the murder of Morgan, as discussed in chapter 4. There were confessions from individuals regarding this means of homicide with purposive disposal of the body (to wit, those of Valance, Giddins and Mann). No matter how near to the truth this explanation seems, there have been no remains recovered from the Niagara River or any adjoining body of water that have been positively identified as those of William Morgan, although we know one body and one skeleton were both temporarily and erroneously (in the case of the body) identified as such. Keep in mind, as mentioned earlier, that the Niagara River was dragged repeatedly, starting soon after Morgan's disappearance and continuing for several months, as Knight describes in 1950. The banks of the river and the shores of nearby Lake Ontario were searched regularly as well.

Along the same line of reasoning, if Morgan was set adrift aboard a canoe and sent over the falls (no. 11), as Hopkins suggested, there were no remains ever reported to have been recovered, either of a body or a watercraft.

MORGAN RETURNS TO SEA AND REINVENTS HIMSELF, DIES IN 1864

The final possibility regarding Morgan's fate is an interesting amalgam of all other themes and, again, does not discount or discredit Whitney's testimony. In addition, it is the only one with any concrete evidence and warrants further investigation (no. 13). It also does not conflict with Whitney's allegations that Morgan left Canada via a steamer ship to parts unknown. The suggestion that he sailed to the Cayman Islands and lived out his years nearby has overtones of the other Caribbean-based tale of the Morgan-pirate being hanged in 1838. Looking deeper into the Cayman Islands "lead," we find that Morgan was said to have befriended a ship captain of the *Constance* and headed south from Boston, only to be shipwrecked off the coast of Cuba and evacuated. He ended up on Little Cayman Island, British West Indies, sometime before 1839. The story turns romantic: there, he met Catherine Ann Page and married her. He and Catherine had children and eventually moved to Utila, Honduras, where they remained. Morgan supposedly requested a private burial under a tree on the family property.

The supporting evidence for this "lead" appears in the form of publicly available genealogical information that provides a family tree of William Anthony Morgan and Catherine Page Morgan continuing on to the present day. The timing of the birth of Ward Granthom Morgan (photo available on the WikiTree genealogy website and shown here) in 1832, said to be the son of William Morgan and Catherine Page, does align with the timing of Morgan's mainland disappearance.

Ward Grantham Morgan. *Photograph from WikiTree.com and W. Jackson's novel* The Incredible Death and Revival of William Morgan.

Details about generations of Ward Granthom (or Grantham, spelled alternatively on ancestry websites) Morgan's descendants follow, primarily based in Utila but some having migrated to the United States (e.g., Texas, Louisiana, Florida). Photos, grave photographs and obituaries are displayed on public internet spaces. Thus there exists some evidence that Morgan did not die but went on to live out his life outside the United States. (WikiTree lists 1864 as the year of Morgan's death.)

Among those publicly available records appears a family story from Thelma Etna (Cooper) Morgan, wife of a great-grandchild of William Morgan named Peter Hardee Morgan Sr. This recollection of family oral history references William Morgan's notably odd behavior when ships came to shore:

> *Mr. Morgan was married in the United States. He must have been a fisherman or some other trade. A friend of his told him that as he left shore, a man was sleeping with his wife. That night he said goodbye as usual,* [and] *when he thought she was asleep, he went home and found her in bed with a said man. He told the man to leave, then he shot his wife and left for sea. He landed in Utila Island.*
>
> *After a short while he married, he told his wife what he had done, it left him a nervous wreck. Whenever a boat was seen coming into the harbors he would go to the bush and hide. His wife knew his hiding place and would take food to him. He stayed until the boat left and was out of sight.*
>
> *His wife bore him a son named Ward Morgan and two daughters, Leticia and Emma. Ward also had a nervous problem. Ward Morgan was a Christian; he was never an excellent preacher, but he exhorted in the Methodist church. He lived a holy, sanctified life. He only knew one woman, a very devoted man.*[79]

Can scientific methods be applied to validate or invalidate the genealogical information that appears on Ancestry or WikiTree? An investigative trend began very recently involving the use of publicly available genealogical data where investigators are able to review family trees as well as actual DNA sequences in order to find possible relatives of the contributor of their unknown sequence(s). In short, genealogical data has become a useful investigative tool. The case of the Golden State Killer serves as an excellent example.

If one looks at William Morgan's own family tree, we know from the historical case narrative that he had two very young children with Lucinda at the time. His daughter, Lucinda Wesley Morgan, was only two years old when her father disappeared, and Thomas Jefferson (T.J.) Morgan was a mere one year of age at that same time. According to records, both children survived into adulthood, and both had families, so William Morgan had two sets of grandchildren and beyond, one in the United States and one in the Caribbean (if we are to believe that the latter are his as well).

This verified historical genealogical lineage of Lucinda Wesley and Thomas Jefferson "T.J." Morgan and their offspring is useful if the mystery of the Caribbean "lead" is to be solved. If male relatives from the Thomas Jefferson "T.J." Morgan line and the Ward Granthom Morgan line allow for their Y chromosome DNA to be tested, then the hypothesis that these two lineages are derived from one male ancestor—William Morgan—would be scientifically verified. If enough loci of the Y chromosome were to be sequenced, then this could be definitively shown.

The lineage of the New York Morgans (children of Lucinda) settled in the western United States (Oregon) with three male grandchildren, named William, James and James. These descendants of Lucinda are less helpful for our scientific investigation since their Y chromosome DNA will have been contributed by their father, not Lucinda (the Morgan connection). Decades of molecular biology research have shown that certain parts of the parental contribution of nuclear DNA passed on to offspring from one parent or the other: mitochondrial DNA, for example, is passed down via the mother, while Y chromosome DNA (the genetic determinant of male sex) is contributed by the father to the male offspring alone.

Thus, the children of T.J.—who, according to census data, married Sarah Jane Day and resided in Eminence, Missouri—could help solve the mystery. The 1860 census from Jasper, Missouri, lists children Louisa (age seven), Sarah (age four) and William (age three). William's Y chromosome DNA and that of any of his male descendants would be crucial to be compared to that of the male descendants from Ward G. Morgan. Unfortunately, at the time of this writing, the census trail for William is not traceable. Yet further research could determine whether William had male offspring who could, today, be compared to the Caribbean Morgan line.

According to online ancestry data, the Caribbean Morgans stayed in Honduras (Utila), and some migrated to the southern and southwestern United States (Texas, Louisiana, California). Three male great-great-grandchildren (Peter H. Jr, James D. and Alfred) are listed on WikiTree.

An excerpt from a 2001 Texas newspaper article elaborates on one of the Caribbean Morgan family members:

> *Etna Thelma Morgan, age 92, of San Antonio, died Thursday, July 26, 2001. She was born in Utila, Honduras. Mrs. Morgan was an active member of Shepherd of the Hills Church of God. She was preceded in death by her husband, Peter Hardy Morgan, Sr. Survivors: sons, Dr. James Morgan and wife, Anita, Peter H. Morgan Jr. and wife, Mary,*

> *and Rev. Alfred Morgan and wife, Febe; daughter, Lillian J. Henderson; brother, Stephen Cooper; sister, Frankie Cooper; 17 grandchildren; 30 great grandchildren; 5 great-great grandchildren; numerous nephews and nieces. SERVICE FRIDAY 1:00 P.M. PORTER LORING CHAPEL The Rev. Dr. James D. Morgan and the Rev. Alfred Morgan officiating.*
>
> *The family invites you to leave a message or memory in the Guest Book by going to www.porterloring.com and clicking on Remembrance Registry. Interment in San Fernando Cemetery III. Arrangements with Porter Loring Mortuary.*

A "historical fiction" book by William Jackson of Utila, Honduras, *The Death and Incredible Revival of William Morgan* (2007), resurrects the story. According to Jackson, local lore tells of Morgan being one of the first to ship bananas to the United States. The love affair with Catherine Page is also highlighted and reiterated. An interesting book review dated October 7, 2018, by J. St. Martin, a self-described "Morgan descendant," states that William Morgan and Catherine Page were his paternal fourth-great-grandparents. This would be another candidate for Y chromosome testing to answer the question of Morgan's fate.

In the past, blood samples of available family members would be required for comparisons to be made; however, today, the process is less invasive and much easier. A buccal swab, taken by scraping a long Q-tip along the inner side of the cheek, produces enough cells for a full DNA sample to be sequenced in the laboratory. Male relatives or purported relatives of William Morgan today could potentially resolve the coldest case in New York State with a simple cotton swab and a mere flick of the wrist.

Chapter 7

SCIENCE AND POLITICS

Sorting Out Sense from Sensibility

So far, this book has explored in detail the case of a missing person—an apparent charlatan, William Morgan—to illustrate how external historical and sociopolitical forces can derail, distract and disrupt the ideally neutral, objective and systematic undertaking of science. This case should serve as an exemplary warning to us all today, as citizens and consumers of information, scientific or otherwise. We saw the push and pull between objective, empirically based observational science and the sociopolitical interpretations of the resulting evidence reported from those observations. In this case, these powerful forces of the collective conscience, driven and shaped by sociopolitical forces as well as by solitary individuals with the power to shape public narratives were at play in 1826 and 1827, resulting in a false positive identification, where the badly decomposed remains of Mr. Timothy Munro were temporarily identified as those of Morgan. Only when (1) Munro's next of kin and friend appeared on the scene with highly detailed information about his physical appearance and personal effects and (2) a third, more thorough, invasive and more scientific coroner's inquest was performed was this erroneous identification corrected.

A second public misidentification came over a half century later in 1881, when a skeleton along with some curious yet highly specific artifacts were uncovered from a Genesee County quarry and the bones were identified as William Morgan's. According to Keene in 2011, ultimately these remains were determined to not be those of Morgan, yet no public announcement of this was made.

Although no report has been discovered on the 1881 skeletal remains from Pembroke, it appears that objective observations ultimately were relied on to determine that the remains were not those of William Morgan, again according to Keene, writing in 2011. However, the haze of writing, talk, rumor and human factors/interpretation that had settled in as a fog in 1827 to obscure public opinion and drastically alter the nation's course again rose in 1881. This time, the opaque mist of conjecture covered the unverified "evidence" found by the Pembroke quarry workers, slandering a deceased individual (Henry Brown), along with purporting some sort of closure to this mysterious cold case. We see that the National Christian Association of Chicago's fervently anti-Masonic leader had his own aspirations, eyeing the future 1884 presidential election. Was public sentiment, the *conscience collective*, once again being molded by those who sought to take control from the current (Freemason) president, James Garfield? Even as recently as 2008, a news article erroneously notes that the Pembroke skeleton "solved" the Morgan cold case and, in so doing, implies that the murder narrative was fact.

In the end, to this day, the Morgan case remains unsolved, since no body has ever been found that has been identified. Chapter 6 makes recommendations as to potential scientific avenues to follow so that the strongest lead can be pursued and, potentially, the case can be closed. It is important to add here that if one were to consult with the internet only on the Morgan case, it would appear to be solved, since his "grave marker ID number" is provided on Find a Grave. Adding to the confusion are journalists who do partial investigations of their own and fail to ask critical questions of previously reported stories and historical narratives. With the application of modern methods, knowledge and context, the case of Morgan as a victim becomes much less apparent. Given what has been gleaned from historical inquiry and follow-up interviews and analyses, one can even rightly question the crimes that were historically attributed to the four who stood trial: Was William Morgan really "kidnapped"? Was he really "falsely imprisoned"?

With this lengthy example, it is clearer than ever—hopefully—to practitioners and the public alike that the scientific process is and always has been one performed by people and thus we can never expect perfect objectivity and neutrality. As technologies improve in order to refine and enhance our senses, it is still up to humans to interpret the results and output of these instruments and machines applied to evidence. As scientists learn during their exposure to the scientific method, all individuals have biases that they bring with them in all that they do. As mentioned earlier, *human factors* is the cognitive psychological term for these conscious and unconscious biases we as humans bring to our work, as we focus on being open-minded, objective and neutral. The studies conducted by Dror (e.g., those of 2006 and 2020) have shown the power of human factors (bias) and were referenced previously in order to make this case.

Happily, the forensic science community has taken note. Awareness that there is a problem is the first step in correcting it. Cognitive science studies, in part, reflect the working context of forensic analysts. Our laboratories and field investigation units exist in a societal context, with overarching political powers giving and taking away resources, setting goals and expectations and requiring outcomes and "deliverables": e.g., so many identifications per year, more reliance on one (cheaper) form of data/analysis over another more expensive one, etc. Scientists never work in a vacuum. Even the scientists in the vaunted "ivory tower" of academia are beholden to campus politics as well as state, national and international research trends and interests. A scientific project will receive no external or internal grant monies if there is no interest from funding sources. Keep in mind that governments (political bodies) oftentimes fund research, picking and choosing which topics are important to research and fund for the current day. Needless to say, funding is the lifeblood of research, and without financial support, most research will progress little or not at all.

Yet it is clear from our historical case example how detrimental to neutrality and objectivity such political forces can be. How are scientists themselves and consumers of scientific information supposed to wade through the mercurial sensibilities of the political waters to use their objective senses in order to be make valid and reliable decisions and to be informed in an accurate and "real" way? We have laid out this book in a way that guides us through the political blur of the storm so that we, whether we be scientists or just consumers of scientific information, can try to see the scientific light.

Reliance on only empirical evidence is strongly encouraged—that is, only what we can touch, see, hear, smell or taste and thus *measure*, in the broadest sense of that term. Thus we apply first and foremost the philosophy of empiricism, that is, the practice of relying on observation and experimentation, especially in the natural sciences. To reiterate from chapter 1, empiricism as a philosophical theory proposes that all knowledge originates in experience. Being able to detect something with our own senses allows us to confirm or deny the reports and interpretations of others. We see this as the gold standard for scientists, and Dror's study shows that even reliance on our senses can be confounded when it comes to decision-making and interpretation based on them.

Yet for scientists as well as day-to-day citizens who are increasingly laden with information, both scientific and nonscientific, our first line of inquiry must be our senses in order to "vet" information quality. In Morgan's case, the citizens involved directly with the missing persons situations could use empiricism in their family members' cases. For Morgan, in 1827, a body, albeit decomposing, was laid before family and friends, its identity to be confirmed or denied based on physical, tangible remains. The second inquest showed that individuals' senses were frustrated or eclipsed by external, powerful forces. Later, a skeleton found not far from Morgan's hometown, supposedly along with personal effects, was linked to him and his disappearance. Again, in 1881, the lack of attention to the remains themselves and the reliance on personal effects to "close" a case was anti-scientific and biased. It is fairly easy to see that the background efforts of anti-Masonic forces were at play nearby, with statue-building and presidential aspirations.

The use of empiricism as the gold standard of obtaining knowledge is impractical, however. We cannot handle and observe all that we hear, read and learn about. What are we to do in this twenty-first-century world of immediate communications and information sharing? Another epistemological approach can assist us vetting information: that is, skepticism.

For additional protection as an observer and investigator, the philosophy of skepticism is recommended. To recap from chapter 1, skepticism is an ancient philosophy, like empiricism, that advocates for an attitude of doubt or a disposition to incredulity either in general or toward a particular object. It proposes that true knowledge or knowledge in a particular area is uncertain. Skeptics recommend the use of suspended judgment, systematic doubt or criticism when one is presented with any information. The use of skepticism as a backup position to empiricism can allow scientists, as well as the general public, to assess data, information, evidence, etc. presented to them with a critical and quality-oriented perspective. This process may take more time than we are used to taking; however, it permits us to screen and filter unreliable and flawed information and protect ourselves from misinformation and unreliable and invalid data.

Let's review the empirical-skeptical approach that we have de facto taken to the missing persons case presented. First, as any cold case investigator will do:

Ancient skeptic Timon of Phlius. Be Timon! *Image license provided by Alamy.com.*

(1) Take in all the background information that can be found on the topic at hand (chapters 1 and 5).

This can be extremely time-consuming, especially with cases or subjects that have been under investigation and researched thoroughly through years or even decades. In the day and age of digital media, investigators may find this information-gathering phase challenging, since some or even the majority of the prior research may not be in digital format. Nonetheless, all the earlier information that can be gathered and read will give the investigator, the researcher, the student (generally speaking, the consumer of the information) the ability to understand the overall picture of the "problem" (as we call it in science). After this background is absorbed, an investigator using the empirical and skeptical approaches must attempt to:

(2) Understand all the scientific data and evidence that has been brought to bear on the topic (chapters 2 and 5).

There may be very little or no such data and evidence available to the researcher, or there may be much to review. No matter its form, it should be considered neutral and objective in its raw form, without absolute credence given to the interpretations (if any are given). For example, in chapter 2, we provided the outcomes of three coroners' inquests regarding remains found in Lake Ontario, Orleans County, New York. We reviewed the evidence and the processes of identification but did not assume any of the inquests' results were correct or valid. The facts spoke for themselves (res gestae).

The scientific, physical evidence all now considered, it is imperative to take a step back in time and:

(3) Attempt to comprehend the political context surrounding the incident and prior work done on it (chapter 3).

This may seem like unnecessary dabbling in history that has little or nothing to do with scientific research and evidence and data collection. But nothing could be further from the truth. The forces at work in society that vie for control and power over people, funds and policy at all levels—local, municipal, state and federal—affect, like it or not, the decisions of scientists and investigators. Witness, as we did, the effect of the misidentification of Timothy Munro and how, like an ember in a dry forest, it crackled into a raging political fire from the backwoods town of Batavia, New York, to the northeast region of the United States, becoming a movement and the "first third" national political party known to this country. Keep in mind that the erroneous identification of Munro had long since been corrected with the third inquest of 1827, yet the political wildfire of anti-Masonry was loathe to be extinguished for years to come. It was the political atmosphere overarching these cases that dictated not the scientific result but the societal acceptance of a result.

With the political context as a backdrop considered, the investigator must take the next step:

(4) Consider the counter-information to the scientific data and evidence presented in step 2 (chapter 4).

This can be done at this stage, since the researcher/investigator will now understand the political forces at work that may have affected the understanding of citizens and consumers of information at the time in question. What information was there to consider besides the scientific evidence or data? What could have pulled a person's belief or understanding away from reliance on scientifically derived, physical, tangible evidence? What were the sources of information, and were they reliable (the two-pronged test for vetting third-party information, considering the totality of circumstances)? If scientists can be affected by unconscious biases, certainly nonscientists would be similarly affected. In the case of William Morgan, actual confessions to the man's murder were provided to courts and officials. Could these be disregarded out of hand? As we asked in chapter 4, why would any person confess to murder if he or she did not commit the act? We must understand the overall political and societal, even psychological, context in order to answer that question.

Finally, with due reflection on the counter-information available about the case being considered, one then must:

(5) Assemble the scientific evidence and counter-information/evidence to form a decision on the case/problem, if possible. (As skeptics would suggest, suspension of judgment/decision is a very viable option if the evidence does not seem to be convincing.)

This is a process that may be facilitated by creating a table or matrix so that evidence can be weighed against counter-evidence. Weight must be given to physical, tangible (that is, empirical and a posteriori) evidence over the nonphysical, nontangible (that is, a priori) information. In the case of Morgan, the leads that emerged after his disappearance were considered with little to no solid data to be had, except for the suggestion that he reestablished himself in the Cayman Islands and ultimately in Honduras. Recommendations based on modern, scientific, Y chromosome or other DNA techniques were made in order to find an answer to the question.

THIS EMPIRICAL AND SKEPTICAL approach to information vetting was used in this case in order to demonstrate the effects of external factors, such as politics, on the scientific undertaking and to suggest a process of information filtering and vetting that allows for open-minded, historically contextualized decision-making. This five-step analytical thought process is more time-consuming than reading a headline and forming a judgment and may even require the use of paper-based literature, much to the chagrin of the digital natives of the world (an ever-growing part of the population). Yet time is what is required to make an informed, empirically based decision relying on our senses, not our sensibilities.

The scientific process uses our observational senses—that is, our visual, acoustic, tactile, olfactory and, yes, even taste skills—to measure the world around us. Yet as humans, we perform these observations within the broader context of society with all its permutations. We have additional, nonobservational faculties at work within and around us every day: that is, our sensibilities. These feelings and emotions affect our senses and the judgments and decisions we make. Scientists work to subdue conscious biases based on such human factors that are known to us and that we can be aware of. Dror's cognitive science work on human factors highlights the great importance of and need for this awareness. Scientists know that is impossible to reduce all these sensibilities to nothing; however, we can be aware of them and consciously try to avoid their entrance into our observations and judgments by wariness and constant cross-checking of our mental thought processes and the written work that emerges from those processes. Having peers review our work is another form of cross-checking. (Keep in mind that there is much "groupthink" within organizations, so this may not work as well as one might hope.)

It is hoped that the reader will be able to see in this missing persons case how sensibilities can obfuscate the judgment of investigators, medical professionals and citizens alike such that relatively clear-cut evidence is avoided, discredited or ignored. A critique of this book could come from its reliance on a case study for its data rather than aggregate data with statistical power. However, a solitary case was used purposefully here in order to demonstrate the impact that one case can have on the larger society. From the mysterious circumstances of William Morgan's disappearance, an entire national political movement evolved. It lasted for a decade, long after the misidentified remains of Timothy Munro were correctly and positively identified and buried in Canada.

It is not, then, the number of cases or the amount of scientific evidence that necessarily impacts the consumers of information—that is, the greater society of citizens. It is rather the use, or abuse, of the information provided to those with a megaphone, a mouthpiece, a soapbox. It is clearly no coincidence that the entire Morgan affair began with William Morgan's alliance with David Miller, a man with the professional ability to print flyers, reports, books and other media. Recall, too, that Thurlow Weed was a New York State politician and owner/editor of a newspaper in Rochester, then Albany, New York. Undoubtedly, his media control affected public information and thus the "knowledge" generated from such information. He could promote stories (e.g., "Morgan's Body Found") and simultaneously ignore others (e.g., "Timothy Munro Remains Identified in Genesee County after Third Inquest").

A single case can have a profound impact on society; this point is clear. Yet as Morris wisely stated in 1883, the embers of belief and acceptance require aeration in order to kindle. Consumers of information of any sort are thus beholden to the information purveyors, who, as we have seen, oftentimes have their own interests in mind. The foregoing chapters have detailed a case and demonstrated an investigative approach to information vetting that can be applied by the individual recipients of information. The epistemological philosophies of empiricism and skepticism are strongly recommended so as to filter evidence, data and information obtained from third party sources.

For our case at hand, we now may have a way to get past rumor and hearsay, since scientific methods exist today that can, once and for all, solve the mystery of William Morgan's fate. If available descendants of T.J. and William Granthom Morgan are located and are amenable to contributing a DNA sample for comparison, then we could be certain of William Morgan's having continued his life in the Caribbean or not. If there exists a consistent Y chromosome or other relevant DNA profile between the two lines, we can conclude that Morgan did carry on with his life in Utila, Honduras. If the two Y chromosome or other relevant DNA profiles do not show consistency, then we can safely conclude that the William Granthom Morgan line is not related to William Morgan of Batavia, New York, and we have "lost his trail," at least for the moment but perhaps forever.

NOTES

Introduction

1. Dror et al., "Contextual Information," 74–78.

Chapter 1

2. Knight, *Strange Disappearance*, 228.
3. Morris, *William Morgan*, 58–59.
4. Brown, *Anti-Masonic Excitement*, 16.
5. Morris, *William Morgan*, 59.
6. Knight, *Strange Disappearance*, 30.
7. Morris, *William Morgan*, 68.
8. Morris, *William Morgan*, 69.

Chapter 2

9. Morris, *William Morgan*, 254.
10. Morris, *William Morgan*, 254.
11. Morris, *William Morgan*, 255.
12. Mock, *Morgan Episode*, 55.
13. Morris, *William Morgan*, 255.

14. Morris, *William Morgan*, 255.
15. Morris, *William Morgan*, 255.
16. Mock, *Morgan Episode,* 55.
17. Palmer, *Morgan Affair*, 23.
18. Morris, *William Morgan,* 259.
19. Morris, *William Morgan*, 259.
20. Morris, *William Morgan*, 259–60.
21. Knight, *Strange Disappearance*, 54.
22. Mock, *Morgan Episode,* 55.
23. Knight, *Strange Disappearance*, 192.
24. Morris, *William Morgan*, 263–64.
25. Morris *William Morgan*, 264.
26. Morris, *William Morgan*, 265.
27. Morris, *William Morgan*, 265.
28. Morris, *William Morgan*, 265.
29. Palmer, *Morgan Affair*, 23.
30. Palmer, *Morgan Affair*, 199.

Chapter 3

31. Palmer, *Morgan Affair*, 197.
32. Morris, *William Morgan*, 45.
33. Morris, *William Morgan*, 45.
34. Morris, *William Morgan*, 45.
35. Morris, *William Morgan*, 46.
36. Morris, *William Morgan*, 46.
37. Creason, "Famous Freemason."
38. Morris, *William Morgan*, 47.
39. History Channel, "Secret Societies," 30.
40. Palmer, *Morgan Affair*, 200.

Chapter 4

41. Stone, *Letters on Masonry*, 293–94.
42. Knight, *Strange Disappearance*, 180–81.
43. Knight, *Strange Disappearance*, 177.
44. Knight, *Strange Disappearance*, 179.

45. Knight, *Strange Disappearance*, 180.
46. Giddins, *1829 Anti-Masonic Almanac*, 21.
47. Giddins, *1829 Anti-Masonic Almanac*, 21.
48. Morris, *William Morgan*, 199.
49. Knight, *Strange Disappearance*, 181.
50. Knight, *Strange Disappearance*, 183.
51. Knight, *Strange Disappearance*, 183.
52. Emery, *Confession*, 10.
53. Emery, *Confession*, 24.
54. Emery, *Confession*, 24–25.
55. Knight, *Strange Disappearance*, 269.
56. Knight, *Strange Disappearance*, 269–71.
57. Kassin and Wrightsman, *Confession Evidence*, 76.
58. Aebi and Campistol, *Voluntary False Confessions*, 194.
59. Aebi and Campistol, *Voluntary False Confessions*, 196.
60. Kassin and Wrightsman, *Confession Evidence*, 76.
61. Aebi and Campistol, *Voluntary False Confessions*, 196–97.
62. "Deathbed Confessions," 253–54.
63. *State v. Dickinson*, 41, 299, 303 (Wisconsin).

Chapter 5

64. Signor, *Landmarks*, 23.
65. Wheaton Archives, 143 papers of Charles Finney.

Chapter 6

66. Voorhis, *What Really Happened*, 261.
67. Morris, *William Morgan*, 65.
68. Morris, *William Morgan*, 65.
69. Morris, *William Morgan*, 66.
70. Morris, *William Morgan*, 67.
71. Morris, *William Morgan*, 67–68.
72. Morris, *William Morgan*, 65.
73. Morris, *William Morgan*, 65.
74. Morris, *William Morgan*, 66–67.
75. Knight, *Strange Disappearance*, 231.

76. Stone, *Letters on Masonry*, 258.
77. Morris, *William Morgan*, 65.
78. Morris, *William Morgan*, 65.
79. Anonymous comment on www.ancestry.com, July 6, 2019.

BIBLIOGRAPHY

Aebi, Marcelo F., and Claudia Campistol. "'Voluntary' False Confessions as a Source of Wrongful Convictions: The Case of Spain." In *Wrongful Convictions and Miscarriages of Justice: Causes and Remedies in North American and European Criminal Justice Systems*, edited by C. Ronald Huff and Martin Killias. Taylor & Francis, 2013.

Anonymous. *A Narrative of the Facts and Circumstances Relating to the Kidnapping and Presumed Murder of Wm. Morgan*. Edwin Scranton, 1827.

Arntfield, Michael, and Michael Arntfield. "'The Mystery of Marie Rogêt': Holdback Evidence and the Copycat Effect." *Gothic Forensics: Criminal Investigative Procedure in Victorian Horror & Mystery* (2016): 79–103.

Batavia Daily News. "Morgan's Monument: The Unveiling Ceremony." September 14, 1882.

———. "A Startling Discovery: The Mystery Solved at Last." June 21, 1881.

Bede, Elbert. "The Morgan Affair and Anti-Masonic Movement." https://oregonscottishrite.wordpress.com/2020/05/28-the-morgan-affair.pdf.

Bernard, David. *Light on Masonry: A Collection of All the Most Important Documents on the Subject of Speculative Free Masonry: Embracing the Reports of the Western Committees in Relation to the Abduction of William Morgan* […] *with All the Degrees of the Order Conferred in a Master's Lodge*. W. Williams, 1829.

Beyer, Bradford J. "False Confessions from the Viewpoint of Federal Polygraph Examiners." ProQuest Dissertations Publishing, 2016.

Bittner, Margo S. *The Legend of Appleton Hall as Told by Margo Sue Bittner*. Winery at Marjim Manor.

British Medical Journal no. 1,488 (1889): 253–54. Deathbed confession.

Brown, Henry. *A Narrative of the Anti-Masonic Excitement in the Western Part of the State of New-York, During the Years 1826, 1827, 1828, and Part of 1829*. Vol. 7. Carey, Lea & Carey, 1830.

Buswell Library Special Collections. National Christian Association (NCA) Records. Vol. SC-29 2008.

Creason, Todd E. "Famous Freemason: Marquis de Lafayette." *Midnight Freemasons* (blog). 2011. http://www.midnightfreemasons.org/2011/07/famous-freemason-marquis-de-lafayette_26.html.

Davis, Michael A. "Life, Death and Masonry—The Body of William Morgan." *Thanatos* 2, no. 1 (2013).

DeSmit, Scott. "Genesee's Oldest, Coldest Case Solved at Last." *Batavia Daily News*, February 16, 2008.

Dror, Itiel E. "Cognitive and Human Factors in Expert Decision Making: Six Fallacies and the Eight Sources of Bias." *Analytical Chemistry* 92, no. 12 (2020): 7,998–8,004.

Dror, Itiel E., David Charlton and Ailsa E. Péron. "Contextual Information Renders Experts Vulnerable to Making Erroneous Identifications." *Forensic Science International* 156, no. 1 (2006): 74–76. https://doi.org/10.1016/j.forsciint.2005.10.017.

"Evidence: Admissibility of Dying Declarations in Other than Homicide Cases." *Michigan Law Review* 25, no. 6 (1927): 673–74.

Evidence—Dying Declarations—Admissibility in Civil Cases. Vol. 12. University of Oregon, 1932.

FamilySearch. "Ward Grantham Morgan." https://ancestors.familysearch.org/en/L6QF-XK4/ward-grantham-morgan-1832-1913.

Farr, Andrew. "William Anthony Morgan (Abt. 1774–Abt. 1864)." https://www.wikitree.com/wiki/Morgan-17741.

Find a Grave. "Database and Images, Memorial Page for William Morgan (1774–1826), Find a Grave Memorial ID 10220283 Citing Batavia Cemetery, Batavia, Genesee County, New York, USA; Maintained by Laurie (Contributor 2811407)." https://www.findagrave.com/memorial/10220283/william-morgan.

Finney, Charles. Collection of 143 papers. Wheaton College. https://archives.wheaton.edu/repositories/4/resources/763.

Formisano, Ronald P. "Populist Currents in the 2008 Presidential Campaign." *Journal of Policy and History* 22, no. 2 (2010): 237–55.

Formisano, Ronald P., and Kathleen Smith Kutolowski. "Antimasonry and Masonry: The Genesis of Protest, 1826–1827." *American Quarterly* 29, no. 2 (1977): 139–65.

Freemason's Chronicle. "The Morgan Mystery." June 25, 1881.

Fully, Georges. "Une Nouvelle Méthode De Détermination De La Taille." *Annales De Médicine Légale Et De Criminologie* 36 (1956): 266–73.

Gallivan, Peter. "Genesee County Masonic Mystery Linked to Niagara County Ghost Story." WGRZ. October 13, 2020. https://www.wgrz.com/article/entertainment/television/programs/daybreak/unknown-part-2/71-6d35e6c2-9f97-47d9-9777-064974c7d71c.

Giddins, Edward. "My Own Adventures in Masonry." In *No. 2, the Anti-Masonic Almanac for the Year of the Christian Era: 1829*. E. Scranton, 1828.

Glaubitz, Nicola. "Counting (on) Crime in De Quincey and Poe: Seriality, Crime Statistics, and the Emergence of a Mass Literary Market." *Nineteenth-Century Serial Narrative in Transnational Perspective, 1830s–1860s: Popular Culture—Serial Culture* (2019): 175–90.

Guiteau, Charles Julius. *The Truth, and the Removal.* Harvard Law School Library. Charles Guiteau, 1882.

Guttmacher, Manfred Schanfarber, and Henry Weihofen. *Psychiatry and the Law.* 1st ed. W.W. Norton, 1952.

Hammond, Jabez D. *The History of Political Parties in the State of New York, from Ratification of the Federal Constitution to December 1840*. Halls, Mills, 1852.

Hartman, Andrew. *A War for the Soul of America: A History of Culture Wars.* University of Chicago Press, 2019.

Hough, Franklin B. *The New York Civil List: Containing the Names and Origin of the Civil Divisions, and the Names and Dates of Election or Appointment of the Principal State and County Officers from the Revolution to the Present Time.* Weed, Parsons, 1858.

Kassin, Saul M. *Confession Evidence.* Vol. 35. Thousand Oaks, CA: Sage Publications, 2008. https://doi.org/10.1177/0093854808321557.

———. *The Psychology of Confession Evidence.* Vol. 52. American Psychological Association, 1997.

Kassin, Saul M., and Lawrence S. Wrightsman. "Confession Evidence." In *Psychology of Evidence and Trial Procedure.* Edited by Saul M. Kassin and Lawrence S. Wrightsman. Sage Publications, 1985.

Keene, Michael. *Folklore and Legends of Rochester: The Mystery of Hoodoo Corner and Other Tales.* The History Press, 2011.

Klugman, Robert H. "Some Factors Affecting the Admissibility of Dying Declarations." *Journal of Criminal Law and Criminology (1931–1951)* 39, no.

5 (1949): 646–50. https://doi.org/10.2307/1138106. https://www.jstor.org/stable/1138106.

Knight, Thomas Arthur. *The Strange Disappearance of William Morgan*. Self-published, 1932.

Kopley, Richard. "The Mystery of Marie Rogêt" and "Various Newspaper Files." In *Edgar Allan Poe and the Dupin Mysteries*. Palgrave Macmillan, 2008.

Krzewinski, Lisa M. *But I Didn›t Do It: Protecting the Rights of Juveniles during Interrogation*. Vol. 22. Boston College Law School, 2002.

Lersen, Sharon. "Does Old Letter Shed Light on Morgan Case?" *Batavia Daily News*, July 25, 1981.

Levin, Mark R. *Unfreedom of the Press*. New York: Threshold Editions, 2019.

Machiavelli, Nicolo. *The Prince*. Translated by George Bull. Penguin Classics, 2003.

Manouvrier, L. *La Détermination De La Taille D'Après Les Grands Os Des Membres: Extrait Des Mémoires De La Société D›Anthropologie De Paris.* 2e Série, T. IV. (S. 347-402, 5 Tabb.) Masson, 1892.

McCann, J.T., A. Reifman, S.M. Kassin and Joseph T. McCann. *Broadening the Typology of False Confessions*. Vol. 53. American Psychological Association, 1998. https://doi.org/10.1037/h0092165.

Medina Tribune. "Masonic Lesson." June 25, 1881.

Méndez, P., L. Junquera and L. Gallego. "Double Teeth." *British Dental Journal* 202, no. 9 (2007): 508–9. doi:10.1038/bdj.2007.413.

Mock, Stanley. *The Morgan Episode in American Freemasonry*. Roycroft, 1930.

Morgan, Oliver, Morris Tidball-Binz and Dana Van Alphen. "Chapter 6, Identification of Dead Bodies." In *Management of Dead Bodies after Disasters: A Field Manual for First Responders*. Pan American Health Organization (PAHO), 2006.

Morgan, Captain William [pseud.]. "Masonic Murder of Captain William Morgan (1826)." *CaptainMorgan1826* (blog), January 11, 2012. https://captainmorgan1826.blogspot.com/2011/12/masonic-murder-of-captain-william.html.

Morgan, William, and David Miller. *Illustrations of Masonry by One of the Fraternity Who Has Devoted Thirty Years to the Subject: "God Said, Let There Be Light, and There Was Light."* M. Gardiner 1827.

Morgan, William. *Illustrations of Masonry*. 3rd ed. Printed for the author, 1827.

Morris, Robert. *William Morgan, Or, Political Anti-Masonry: Its Rise, Growth and Decadence.* R. Macoy, 1884.

NC Medical Journal no. 1, 24 (1889). Deathbed confession.

New York Times. "Mystery Solved in Upstate Quarry." June 22, 1881.

———. "A Old Tragedy Revived." September 14, 1882.

Ofshe, Richard J., and Richard A. Leo. *The Decision to Confess Falsely: Rational Choice and Irrational Action*. Vol. 74. University of Denver College of Law, 1997.

Ontario General Sessions. *The Trial of James Lackey, Isaac Evertson, Chauncy H. Coe, Holloway Howard, Hiram Hubbard, John Butterfield, James Ganson, Asa Knowlen, Harris Seymour, Henry Howard, and Moses Roberts, for Kidnapping Capt. William Morgan; at the Ontario General Sessions; Held at Canandaigua, Ontario County, Aug. 22, 1827*. MSU Libraries, 1827.

Orwell, George. *Nineteen Eighty-Four*. Penguin Classics, 1949.

Palmer, John Carpenter. *The Morgan Affair and Anti-Masonry*. Vol. 2. Masonic Service Association of the United States, 1924.

Plato, James Adam, and D.A. Rees. *The Republic of Plato*. Cambridge University Press, 1963.

Poe, Edgar Allen. "The Mystery of Marie Roget." *Snowden's Ladies Companion*, 1845.

Porter Loring Mortuaries. "Etna Thelma Morgan Obituary." https://www.porterloring.com/obituaries/Etna-Thelma-Morgan?obId=18278749.

Ramsey, Scott. "Capt. William Morgan." *Awareness of Nothing* (blog). 2017. www.awarenessofnothing.com/capt-william-morgan.html.

Rollet, Etienne. "Des Os Longs Des Membres De L'Homme (Étude Anthropologique Et Médico-Légale)." *Bulletin De La Société D'Anthropologie De Lyon* 8, no. 1 (1889): 12–37.

Roth, Martin. "Mysteries of 'The Mystery of Marie Rogêt.'" *Poe Studies/Dark Romanticism* 22, no. 2 (1989): 27–34. https://www.jstor.org/stable/45296946.

Secret Societies. The History Channel. Mediaworks Productions, 2022.

Signor, Isaac Smith, and Henry Perry Smith. *Landmarks of Orleans County, New York* [...]. D. Mason, 1894.

Sigurdsson, Jon F., and Gisli H. Gudjonsson. *The Psychological Characteristics of "False Confessors": A Study among Icelandic Prison Inmates and Juvenile Offenders*. Vol. 20. Pergamon, 1996.

Silsby, Robert W. *The Holland Land Company in Western New York*. Buffalo and Erie County Historical Society, 1961.

Sledzik, Paul, and Amy Mundorff. "Forensic Anthropology in Disaster Response." In *Handbook of Forensic Anthropology and Archaeology*. 2nd ed. Edited by S. Blau and D. Ubelaker. Taylor and Francis, 2016.

State v. Dickinson, 41 299, 303 (Wisconsin, 1877).

Stone, William Leete. *Letters on Masonry and Anti-Masonry: Addressed to the Hon. John Quincy Adams*. O. Halsted, 1832.

Theiss, Nancy Stearns. "Freemasons, Death, Intrigue Add Life to History." *Courier Journal*, August 3, 2016. https://www.courier-journal.com/story/news/local/oldham/2016/03/08/freemasons-death-intrigue-add-life-history/81443750.

Twain, Mark. *Adventures of Huckleberry Finn*. William Collins, 2010.

Valance, Henry, and John Emery. *Confession of the Murder of William Morgan as Taken Down by John Emery, M.D.* CreateSpace Independent Publishing Platform, 1848.

Voorhis, H.V. "What Really Happened to William Morgan? A Plausible Story." In *The Morgan Affair and Anti-Masonry*. Edited by John C. Palmer. MaCoy, 1946.

Weed, Thurlow. *Life of Thurlow Weed Including His Autobiography and a Memoir.* Vol. 1. Houghton Mifflin, 1883.

Welbury, Richard, Monty S. Duggal and Marie Thérèse Hosey. *Paediatric Dentistry*. Oxford University Press, 2018.

Wheaton Archives. 143 papers of Charles Finney. https://archives.wheaton.edu.

Whitney, Parkhurst, Timothy Shaw, Noah Beach, William Miller, Samuel M. Chubbuck and Circuit Court New York Special. *Trial of Parkhusrt* [sic] *Whitney, Timothy Shaw, Noah Beach, William Miller, and Samuel M. Chubbuck: For a Conspiracy: The Abduction, False Imprisonment, and Assault and Battery, of William Morgan: Had at a Special Circuit Court, Held at Lockport, Niagara County, Feb. 1831, the Hon. Samuel Nelson, One of the Justices of the Supreme Court, Presiding, Embracing the Testimony, Arguments of Counsel, Judge's Charge, &c.* Published at the Balance Office, 1831.

William Morgan Memorial Digital Library. "The William Morgan Home Page." https://www.olivercowdery.com/morganhome/1873morg.htm.

Wimsatt, William Kurtz. "Poe and the Mystery of Mary Rogers." *PMLA* 56, no. 1 (1941): 230–48.

Wrightsman, Lawrence S., and Saul M. Kassin. "Confession Evidence." In *The Psychology of Evidence and Trial Procedure*. Edited by Saul Kassin and Lawrence Wrightsman. Sage Publications, 1985.

ABOUT THE AUTHOR

Dr. Ann Webster Bunch is a forensic anthropologist who has dedicated her career to missing person searches and methods. After finishing graduate school as an Andean zooarchaeologist, she soon began to apply her academic and field training and knowledge to this facet of investigations, first with the United States government as a search and recovery team member for the United States Army Central Identification Laboratory (USA-CIL) in Hawaii. In the role of team anthropologist, she and other active duty military team specialists were tasked with searching for, recovering and identifying any missing-in-action service member or civilian lost in past conflicts. The majority of her overseas work with USA-CIL was in Southeast Asia. From the MIA searches, Dr. Bunch moved back to her home state of New York, where her forensic expertise now is applied to current medico-legal cases in its central and western regions. This work involves searching for missing persons, recovering skeletal remains, assisting in the identification of unidentified remains and determining manner of death based on skeletal injury patterns.